W9-AGB-961

THE THREE
LANGUAGES
OF POLITICS

THE THREE
LANGUAGES
OF POLITICS

TALKING ACROSS
THE POLITICAL DIVIDES

ARNOLD KLING

Copyright © 2013, 2017, 2019 by Arnold Kling.
All rights reserved.

Third Edition: August 2019.

Print ISBN: 978-1-948647-42-7
Ebook ISBN: 978-1-948647-43-4

Library of Congress Cataloging-in-Publication Data available.

Cover design: Derek Thornton, Faceout Studio.

Printed in Canada.

CATO INSTITUTE
1000 Massachusetts Avenue, NW
Washington, DC 20001
www.cato.org

CONTENTS

Preface to the Third Edition

Our political debates are not debates but are instead vehement expressions of tribal anger.

That insight was the basis for the first edition of this book, which was published in 2013. Since then, the insight has been reinforced. There is now widespread concern with the way that political divisions are exacerbated by the communication that takes place in both traditional and social media. This edition includes an afterword that covers some of this very recent literature related to my theme.

The first edition did not make it sufficiently clear that the three-axes model is meant to describe political psychology and political communication, rather than to dissect political thought. The second edition clarified that.

The second edition made only an offhand mention of the newly emerged phenomenon of Donald Trump. This edition includes a brief chapter about this phenomenon.

Mr. Trump's victory in the 2016 presidential election has stimulated interest in political psychology and political communication. But the insight that drove me to write this book is more durable and less accidental than that electoral outcome.

In short, I will make no claim here to analyze or explain Mr. Trump's political success. But I think my characterizations of political psychology and political communication are certainly apropos in the context of the Trump era.

Preface to the Second Edition

In 2013, I self-published an ebook called *The Three Languages of Politics*. I am pleased that Libertarianism.org has decided to issue a new edition of this work, including a print version. The main theory of political communication in *The Three Languages* remains unchanged. However, I am taking this opportunity to revise the presentation, to include new material, and to show how the theory applies to events that have taken place since 2013.

I would like to thank the following for comments on earlier drafts of this book: Tyler Cowen, Jeffrey Friedman, John Samples, Aaron Ross Powell, and Nick Schulz.

1

The Nature of Political Arguments

> When you can classify a significant movement as unworthy of your consideration due to your intellectual or political station, it is hard to then sit down and work out solutions to shared problems.
>
> —John Mauldin[1]

What are all the newspaper columnists, television talking heads, pajama-clad bloggers, Facebook sharers, and Twitter pundits doing? An individual will make a point that seems totally convincing to the people who agree with him or her. And yet the point leaves those who disagree unaffected. How can that be?

Raise your hand if you think those people are engaged in a constructive process of conversation and deliberation. . . .

I don't see many hands going up.

Americans appreciate the value of cooperation, and we are skilled at it. However, when it comes to politics, politically aware Americans seem to split into tribes, and those tribes use the skills of cooperation not to work with each other, but instead to mobilize against each other.

As human beings, we have the gift of language. We can use that gift to engage in deliberation, as when we sit on a jury. But we can also use that gift to try to solidify coalitions in an attempt to conquer or destroy others.

I have sat on a jury. It was a difficult case, without an obvious verdict to be given. We deliberated for three days. We treated one another with respect. We listened to one another. Many of us changed our minds during the process.

Political discussion can be similarly deliberative. However, recently the trend is in the opposite direction, toward becoming more obstinate and less tolerant of other points of view.

My goal in this book is to encourage people to take the first step toward healthier political discussion. I believe that this first step is to recognize the language of coalition mobilization so that we can resist being seduced by that language. If we recognize when people who agree with us are trying to close our minds and shut down discussion, then we have a chance to participate in a more deliberative process.

My politically interested friends tend to sort themselves into three tribal coalitions—progressive, conservative, and libertarian. Progressives (P) assert a moral superiority over conservatives and libertarians. Conservatives (C) assert a moral superiority over libertarians and progressives. And libertarians (L) assert a moral superiority over progressives and conservatives. They cannot all be correct. And when they think in those terms, it is unlikely that they will sit down and work out solutions to shared problems.

I would like to see political discussion conducted with less tribal animosity and instead with more mutual respect and reasoned deliberation. This book can help you recognize when someone is making a political argument that is divisive and serves no constructive purpose. That person could easily be someone who agrees with you or me on the issues. It might even be you or me.

Humans evolved to send and receive signals that enable us to recognize people we can trust. One of the most powerful signals is that the person speaks our language. If someone can speak like a native, then almost always he or she is a native, and natives tend to treat each other better than they treat strangers.

In politics, I claim that progressives, conservatives, and libertarians are like tribes speaking different languages. The language that resonates with one tribe does not connect with the others. As a result, political discussions do not lead to agreement. Instead, most political commentary serves to increase polarization. The points that people make do not open the minds of people on the other side. They serve to close the minds of the people on one's own side.

Which political language do you speak? Of course, your own views are carefully nuanced, and you would never limit yourself to speaking in a limited language. So think of one of your favorite political commentators, an insightful individual with whom you generally agree. Which of the following statements would that commentator most likely make?

(P): My heroes are people who have stood up for the underprivileged. The people I cannot stand are the people who are indifferent to the oppression of women, minorities, and the poor.

(C): My heroes are people who have stood up for Western values. The people I cannot stand are the people who are indifferent to the assault on the moral virtues and traditions that are the foundation for our civilization.

(L): My heroes are people who have stood up for individual rights. The people I cannot stand are the people who are indifferent to government taking away people's ability to make their own choices.

The central claim of this book is that P is the language of progressives, C is the language of conservatives, and L is the language of libertarians. If the theory is correct, then someone who chooses P tends to identify with progressives, someone who chooses C tends to identify with conservatives, and someone who chooses L tends to identify with libertarians.

I call this the three-axes model of political communication.

- A progressive will communicate along the oppressor-oppressed axis, framing issues in terms of the P dichotomy.

- A conservative will communicate along the civilization-barbarism axis, framing issues in terms of the C dichotomy.

- A libertarian will communicate along the liberty-coercion axis, framing issues in terms of the L dichotomy.[2]

Note that the progressive is not using the phenomenon of oppression per se as a means of expressing a political viewpoint. Rather, the progressive believes that certain groups or classes of people intrinsically fall into categories of oppressor or oppressed. For example, a progressive might readily concede that Fidel Castro committed oppression, but the progressive might be much more reluctant to view Castro as belonging to the category or class of oppressors. On the contrary, some progressives would say that Castro took the side of the oppressed against their oppressors. (If this seems confusing, it is because I am confused about why progressives have sympathized with the Cuban Revolution.)

To use another example, conservatives have complained about their treatment on college campuses, including having conservative speakers "disinvited" from college events or shouted down when they do appear. Conservatives might seek to label such treatment "oppression," but progressives would never agree to categorizing conservatives as belonging to an oppressed class.

Let me quickly add that I do *not* believe that the three-axes model serves to explain or to describe the different political ideologies. I am not trying to say that political beliefs are caused by one's choice of axis. Nor am I saying that people think exclusively in terms of their preferred axis.

What I am saying is that when we *communicate* about issues, we tend to fall back on one of the three axes. By doing so, we engage in political tribalism. We signal to members of our tribe that we agree with them, and we enhance our status in the tribe. However, even though it appears that we are arguing against people from other tribes, those people pay no heed to what we say. It is as if we are speaking a foreign language.

Recently, anthropologist John Tooby summarized coalitional behavior as deeply programmed into human conduct.[3]

> These programs enable us and induce us to form, maintain, join, support, recognize, defend, defect from, factionalize, exploit, resist, subordinate, distrust, dislike, oppose, and attack coalitions. Coalitions are sets of individuals interpreted by their members and/or by others as sharing a common abstract identity.

> Moreover, to earn membership in a group you must send signals that clearly indicate that you differentially support it compared to rival groups. Hence, optimal weighting of beliefs and communications in the individual mind will make it feel good to think and express content conforming to and flattering to one's group's shared beliefs, and feel good attacking and misrepresenting rival groups.

One might also think of the three axes as axes of demonization. For example, when a progressive labels someone a racist, the progressive is putting that person on the oppressor end of the oppressor-oppressed axis. When a conservative labels someone a nihilist, the conservative is putting that person on the barbarism end of the civilization-barbarism axis. When a libertarian labels someone a statist, the libertarian is putting that person on the coercion end of the liberty-coercion axis.

The three axes allow each tribe to assert moral superiority. The progressive asserts moral superiority by denouncing oppression and accusing others of failing to do so. The conservative asserts moral superiority by denouncing barbarism and accusing others of failing to do so. The libertarian asserts moral superiority by denouncing coercion and accusing others of failing to do so.

You will be surprised by how many political issues and news events can be framed in terms of the three axes. You might think that different events would require different frameworks of interpretation. However, it turns out that nearly any event can be interpreted from the perspective of each of the axes. If you stick to your own axis, then every event appears to confirm your point of view while making others' views seem less reasonable.

For example, consider the issue of police conduct in dealing with African Americans that has spawned the movement known as Black Lives Matter. This movement emerged after the first edition of this book was issued. Yet I found that progressives, conservatives, and libertarians tend to interpret Black Lives Matter in terms of their preferred axes.

The progressive framing of the issue emphasizes racism, among police and in society as a whole. Progressives put white police, or white society at large, in the role of oppressors, with African Americans in the role of the oppressed.

The conservative framing of the issue emphasizes the need for order. Conservatives put criminal suspects and unruly demonstrators in the role of barbarian threats and put police in the role of defenders of civilization.

The libertarian framing of the issue emphasizes the need for citizens to be free of police harassment. Libertarians put in the role of coercive agents those lawmakers who criminalize harmless activities, such as recreational drug use, as well as police who employ excessive force, while putting those who are accosted and physically harmed by police in the role of citizens who are denied their rights.

With careful consideration, one can see at least some merit in all three ways of framing the issue. Police have shot African American suspects who were unarmed and not apparently dangerous, and that legitimizes concerns about racism and the oppressor versus oppressed framing. However, some of the highly publicized cases of police shootings were more justified than protestors claimed,[4] and some of the so-called protests have been associated with disorder, such as looting, rioting, and incitement to violence against police. These aspects seem to fit more with civilization versus barbarism. The libertarian view also has merit, as certain laws, such as those against recreational drug use and vagrancy, are responsible for unnecessary confrontations with police, and one can make a case that U.S. police are too highly militarized in their equipment and training. There seems to be too much coercion and not enough respect for liberty.

I encourage readers to adopt slow political thinking, which means seeing an issue from a number of angles rather than along just one axis. In contrast, fast political thinking means settling on a single axis to frame an issue. Readers familiar with psychologist Daniel Kahneman's 2011 book *Thinking, Fast and Slow* will notice that I am borrowing from his terminology. I believe that once you notice the difference between fast political thinking and slow political thinking, you will prefer the latter.

You can use the three-axes model in two ways. First, you can predict how commentators of the three different political persuasions will seek to frame new events. Second, you can slow your own political thinking. You can catch yourself when you start to frame an issue in your preferred language, without considering other nuances. You can become more cautious about your own beliefs and less inclined to dismiss people with whom you disagree as malevolent. You can avoid contributing to polarization and unproductive debates where people simply talk past one another.

Note that I apply the three-axes model to arguments made by politically aware contemporary Americans. The model is not designed to apply to other time periods or other countries.

2

Applying the Three-Axes Model

Consider the following examples of phenomena for which I give three possible reactions. In each case, I use the three-axes model to frame the issues in terms I believe will resonate with conservatives, progressives, or libertarians, respectively. I am not saying that these hypothetical reactions are precisely what people with these different viewpoints would say. However, I predict that conservatives will tend to find my hypothetical conservative interpretations of the phenomena to be the most congenial. Similarly, I expect progressives and libertarians will be inclined to agree with the interpretations that are based on what I think of as their preferred axes.

1. Interpreting the Holocaust, in which Nazis murdered millions of Jews

Along the conservative civilization-barbarism axis, I would offer an explanation that sees the Holocaust as illustrating the evil that people will do when their institutions break down. The Germans were once a civilized people, and they have returned to being a civilized people. However, their defeat in World War I, the punitive Versailles treaty, and the economic traumas of hyperinflation and depression caused Germans to abandon their traditional institutions. Under the spell of the Nazis, the Germans engaged in genocide. To prevent such horrors, we need to make sure that traditional religion and government remain legitimate in the eyes of citizens. Traditional institutions represent civilization. Abandoning traditional institutions leads to barbarism.

Along the progressive oppressor-oppressed axis, I would offer an explanation that sees the Holocaust as an example of the dangers of ethnic prejudice. Genocide is an extreme example of behavior that stems from negative stereotyping of minority groups. Anti-Semitism festered in Germany for many decades, and the Nazis carried it to the extremes. The purveyors of anti-Semitism and other forms of ethnic bias are oppressors. The victims of their prejudice are the oppressed. To prevent such horrors, citizens need to be taught that we are all human beings, in spite of superficial differences in race, gender, and religion.

Along the libertarian liberty-coercion axis, I would offer an explanation that sees the Holocaust as an example of the dangers of putting faith in an all-encompassing state. Totalitarian regimes are willing to commit mass murder to remain in power and to pursue ideological goals. Both Nazis and Communists murdered millions of citizens. To prevent such horrors, we need to preserve liberty and give less power to government.

2. Goals of tax reform

For a conservative along the civilization-barbarism axis, the main priority of tax reform should be to promote traditional values. The tax code should reward hard work, thrift, and married couples with children. Traditional families, hard work, and thrift are elements of civilization. If taxation penalizes civilized behavior and undermines civilized values, then this fosters an eventual return to barbarism.

For a progressive along the oppressor-oppressed axis, the main priority of tax reform should be to reduce inequality. The tax code should extract unwarranted wealth from the rich to provide more public services and assistance to the poor.

For a libertarian along the liberty-coercion axis, the main priority of tax reform should be to limit the size of government. Taxes ought to be minimal. The freedom to dispose of your own wealth as you wish is liberty. Taxes are obtained by coercion.

3. The Israeli-Palestinian conflict

Along the conservative civilization-barbarism axis, the focus is on the way that Israeli values align with American values. Conservatives emphasize the nihilism of Palestinian terrorism. To support Israel is to defend civilization. To support the Palestinians is to promote barbarism.

Along the progressive oppressor-oppressed axis, the focus is on the political and economic adversities faced by the Palestinians. Progressives see Israeli policy as responsible for much of the Palestinian suffering. To support the Palestinians is to stand up for an oppressed people. To support the current policies of Israel is to back the oppressors.

Along the libertarian liberty-coercion axis, the focus is on the corruption of Palestinian government and the militarism of Israel. For the United States, the policy that is most consistent with liberty is one of nonintervention in foreign affairs. Providing diplomatic and financial assistance to Israel requires coercive taxation at home to support a coercive government abroad.

4. A 1992 study by the Federal Reserve Bank of Boston, which found a high rejection rate for mortgage applications by African Americans[5]

From the perspective of the conservative civilization-barbarism axis, mortgage credit should go to people who work hard, save, and handle credit responsibly. Regardless of race, it is appropriate to deny mortgage credit to households unless they have shown an ability to handle credit responsibly. Rewarding virtuous behavior and denying credit to the profligate helps in the contest between civilization and barbarism.

From the perspective of the progressive oppressor-oppressed axis, the Boston Fed study shows that African Americans face discrimination in the mortgage market. It shows a need for government to protect minorities with tougher enforcement of banking regulations. Otherwise, minority families who wish to own homes will be handicapped by the oppressive practices of bankers.

From the perspective of the libertarian liberty-coercion axis, banks should be allowed to make their own lending decisions. Libertarians might suspect that the results of the study were distorted to make it appear that government involvement is warranted.

5. Abortion and unwed motherhood

Conservatives would look at abortion and unwed motherhood from the perspective of the civilization-barbarism axis and say that those phenomena are symptoms of cultural decay. Young people are not learning sexual restraint and the value of marriage the way that they did many decades ago. We need to try to reverse this.

Progressives would look at abortion and unwed motherhood from the perspective of the oppressor-oppressed axis and say that we need to ensure that poor people are given economic opportunity, education, and access to birth control. Unwed mothers are oppressed and deserve our sympathy. Those who would heap blame on unwed mothers or try to limit the availability of abortion are oppressors.

Libertarians would look at abortion and unwed motherhood from the perspective of the liberty-coercion axis and say that government should not be trying to regulate personal behavior. Individual choices about sex, marriage, childbearing, and abortion represent liberty. Government regulation represents coercion.

6. The "war on terror"

Conservatives would say that the threat of Muslim extremism is sufficiently difficult and dangerous to justify the use of surveillance and military power. Conservatives see barbarism both in theocratic Muslim states and in the means used by Muslim extremists. They see a need for our civilization to stand up and defend itself.

Progressives would say that our response to terrorism is based too much on prejudice and that it alienates the people with whom we need to get along. The "war on terror" serves to oppress the vast majority of Muslims who are innocent. Those who exaggerate fears of Muslim terrorism are oppressors.

Libertarians are opposed to government surveillance and targeted killing. Libertarians are skeptical whenever government declares a "war," because this can provide a pretext for curtailing liberty. The "war on terror" involves an unjustified expansion of government coercion.

7. A baker, citing his or her religious views, who refuses to bake a wedding cake for a gay marriage

Conservatives would say that religion is important for civilization. They would argue that the baker's freedom to exercise his or her religion should be protected.

Progressives would view gays as a historically oppressed class. The gay couple's ability to obtain a wedding cake is limited by prejudice. Government must combat this prejudice and ensure that bakers do not refuse to sell wedding cakes to gay couples.

Libertarians would say that government should not become involved in either marriage decisions or cake-baking decisions.[6] People should have a choice in whom they marry.

Cake bakers should not be coerced into baking cakes that they do not wish to bake.

8. Soda taxes

From a conservative point of view, civilized people need to control obesity through self-restraint. It is not the soda itself that is barbaric; it is the people who consume too many calories from all sources.

From a progressive point of view, corporations that market sugary sodas can be thought of as oppressors, and people who become obese in part from drinking soda can be thought of as oppressed. Progressives might view soda taxes as a blow against the oppressors and a benefit to the oppressed.

From a libertarian point of view, it is not the government's job to police calorie intake. Soda taxes represent coercion.

Concerning soda taxes, columnist Catherine Rampell wrote as follows:

> Why not just target the output, rather than some random subset of inputs? We could tax obesity if we wanted to. Or if we want to seem less punitive, we could award tax credits to obese people who lose weight. A tax directly pegged to reduced obesity would certainly be a much more efficient way to achieve the stated policy goal of reducing obesity.[7]

Her droll suggestion is what showed me that the three-axes model applies to this example. Taxing obesity itself would be more in line with the conservative axis. Taxing only soda appeals more to the progressive axis. Neither approach would appeal to the libertarian axis.

In review

These examples illustrate that each of the three languages can be used to frame a wide variety of issues. As a result, you are likely to observe conservatives making arguments and approving of arguments along the civilization versus barbarism axis, and similarly for progressives and libertarians along their respective axes.

As you were reading the examples in this chapter, you might have seen them as simplistic. If so, that is a good sign. It indicates that you are not so steeped in any one viewpoint that you cannot listen to other points of view. Your views are more nuanced than the knee-jerk responses based on the three-axes model. You employed slow political thinking rather than slipping into fast political thinking.

I believe that the three languages of politics are used as part of fast political thinking. The main prescriptive theme of this book is that you should hesitate when you find yourself inclined to frame an issue in terms of your preferred political language. Instead, try to switch over to slow political thinking.

Before proceeding, let me reiterate some key points.

1. I propose that the three dominant moral frames (oppressor-oppressed, civilization-barbarism, and liberty-coercion) are useful in a descriptive sense. I call this the three-axes model. Those moral frames do not necessarily describe how people arrive at their opinions. However, the frames do predict the language that people are likely to use in political communications.

2. I am *not* saying that the ideologies of progressivism, conservatism, and libertarianism can be boiled down to just these three moral frames. Each of those ideological tendencies is in fact complex and multifaceted.

3. Turning from the descriptive to the prescriptive, I believe that linguistic differences and negative stereotypes are dangerous. Politically aware Americans use those frames to assert moral superiority. They take it for granted that once an issue has been framed in their preferred way, it is settled. I believe that each of us can reason more constructively and deliberate more effectively across political tribes if we recognize that we tend to be overly attuned to our preferred language. We can reduce

our level of political anger by better understanding the other languages. While listening to another language, you can still carry the belief that you are right, and you do not need to split differences or compromise. However, you should be less inclined to demonize people who speak different political languages.

For politically engaged Americans today, ideology has become a powerful marker of identity. It is useful to think of progressives, conservatives, and libertarians as rivalrous, hostile tribes. As such, they have developed linguistic differences and negative stereotypes of one another, which the three-axes model can help to articulate. In a tribe, political language is used to assert the moral superiority of one's tribe. Communicating using the preferred axis of the tribe is good for reassuring others of one's loyalty to the tribe, for lifting a person's status in the tribe by pleasing those who agree with him or her, and for whipping up hostility against other tribes. What political language is not good for is persuading people outside one's tribe or improving relations with them.

Fast Political Thinking and Simple Moral Frames

What I call fast political thinking is driven by simplified moral frames. These moral frames give us the sense that those who agree with us have the right answer, while those who disagree are unreasonable, or worse.

Each moral frame sets up an axis of favorable and unfavorable. Progressives use the oppressor-oppressed axis. Progressives view most favorably those groups that can be regarded as oppressed or standing with the oppressed, and they view most unfavorably those groups that can be regarded as oppressors. Conservatives use the civilization-barbarism axis. Conservatives view most favorably the institutions that they believe constrain and guide people toward civilized behavior, and they view most unfavorably those people who they see as trying to tear down such institutions. Libertarians use the liberty-coercion axis. Libertarians view most favorably those people who defer to decisions that are made on the basis of personal choice and voluntary agreement, and they view most unfavorably those people who favor government interventions that restrict personal choice.

If you have a dominant axis, I suggest that you try to learn the languages spoken by those who use the other axes. Don't worry—learning other languages won't make it easy for others to convert you to their point of view. By the same token, it will not make it easy to convert others to your point of view. However, you may become aware of assumptions your side makes that others might legitimately question.

What learning the other languages can do is enable you to understand how others think about political issues. Instead of resorting to the theory that people with other views are crazy or stupid or evil, you may concede that they have a coherent point of view. In fact, their point of view could be just as coherent as yours. The problem is that those people apply their point of view in circumstances where you are fairly sure that it is not really appropriate.

Consider that there may be situations in which one frame describes the problem much better than the others. For example, I believe that the civil rights movement in the

United States is best described using the progressive heuristic of the oppressed and the oppressor. In the 1950s and the early 1960s, the people who had the right model were the people who were fighting for black Americans to have true voting rights, equal access to housing, and an end to the Jim Crow laws. The civilization-barbarism axis and the liberty-coercion axis did not provide the best insight into the issue. In fact, I would argue that among conservatives and libertarians, leading icons such as Barry Goldwater and Milton Friedman took positions that in retrospect were wrong-headed. In his 1962 book *Capitalism and Freedom*, Friedman supported the rights of individuals to discriminate. His view might have been consistent with opposition to government-enforced discrimination, as produced by the Jim Crow laws. However, Goldwater did not even stand up against the Jim Crow laws. Instead, he supported the rights of states to enact such laws against the authority of the federal government.

Conversely, consider the issue of urban crime, which became a major issue in the 1970s. The conservative model of stricter law enforcement and stronger police presence appears to have had some success in reducing urban crime. As a result, it has become much less fashionable than it was in the 1960s to think about crime solely in terms of "root causes" related to oppressed classes.

Finally, consider the criminalization of marijuana. For many decades, this policy was based on the conservative's civilization-barbarism analysis. Marijuana was thought to lead to degeneracy, and therefore it should be outlawed. Increasingly, the libertarian focus along the liberty-coercion axis is gaining sway.

4

Beyond Your Dominant Heuristic

I believe that many issues are more complex than the simple heuristics would suggest. Left to ourselves as individuals, we would arrive at subtle, nuanced views on these issues. However, politics has a very important social dimension. The language we use to convey our positions to others typically does not reveal the nuances and doubts we hold as individuals.

As a social phenomenon, political discussions invite us to position ourselves relative to others. We want to raise our individual status in our own tribe, and we want to reduce the status of other tribes. By framing issues in terms of our preferred axis, we appear to accomplish both of these goals. We impress the people who agree with us, and we delegitimize those who disagree.

However, to the extent that we might like to see discussion lead to improved understanding, our political debates are frustrating and endless. Each tribe expresses itself along its preferred axis. As a result, we talk past one another rather than communicate. Moreover, we have a tendency to demonize those with whom we cannot communicate. Rather than consider that they may have a reasonable point of view, we come to believe that they are our opponents along our preferred axis. Thus, if you are a progressive focused on the oppressor-oppressed axis, you may come to view conservatives and libertarians as being on the side of the oppressors. If you are a conservative focused on the civilization-barbarism axis, you may come to view progressives and libertarians as enemies of civilized values. And if you are a libertarian focused on the liberty-coercion axis, you may come to view progressives and conservatives as champions of coercive government.

Learning to speak other political languages can enable you to look at political debate from a point of view detached from your preferred heuristic. I am not saying that you should give up your preferred heuristic. However, you will find it useful to detach from it on occasion. Detachment can help you understand those who use different heuristics. It also might enable you to employ slow political thinking rather than fast.

Detachment can help us to see the merit in other points of view and avoid taking our own views to erroneous extremes. Detachment can lead us to take a charitable view of others' disagreement, rather than retreating into demonization. Learning the other political languages might help us to have conversations instead of shouting matches.

Cognitive scientist Gary Klein uses the term "decentering." He writes:

> Decentering is not about empathy—intuiting how others might be feeling. Rather, it is about intuiting what others are thinking. It is about imagining what is going through another person's mind. It is about getting inside someone else's head.
>
> . . . Being able to take someone else's perspective lets people disagree without escalating into conflicts.[8]

Taking a charitable view of those with whom we disagree is rare in the political media. Many of the most popular newspaper columnists, radio talk show hosts, bloggers, and pundits using cable TV or social media do exactly the opposite. They take the most *un*charitable view possible of those with whom they disagree, and they encourage their followers to do likewise. They achieve high ratings, but they lower the quality of political discussion. If you have a dominant political language, then chances are that both your favorite public intellectuals and your most hated demagogues are guilty of doing this.

The strategy of being uncharitable focuses on finding the weakest arguments of opponents and denouncing those arguments and characterizing the opponents as having relied entirely on those weak arguments. Often, it involves finding opponents' statements that can be interpreted as justifying a view that the opponent is on the opposite end of one's preferred axis. For example, in 2012, Republican presidential candidate Mitt Romney was recorded saying the following:

> All right, there are 47 percent who are with him, who are dependent upon government, who believe that they are victims, who believe the government has a responsibility to care for them, who believe that they are entitled to health care, to food, to housing, to you-name-it.[9]

Progressive pundits took this statement as confirmation of their view that Romney had no sympathy for the oppressed. I am not suggesting that they should have taken a more charitable view of this remark. However, that they chose to focus on it and to use it to define Romney was a way of taking the least charitable view of his candidacy.

Conversely, during the 2012 Democratic convention, a platform controversy emerged. The original platform conspicuously omitted a reference to God and to Jerusalem as the capital of Israel. When that language was restored on the floor, some delegates were unhappy with the process, and they booed. Conservative pundits portrayed this as the Democrats booing God and Israel, as if this proved that the Democrats had abandoned civilized values and turned into barbarians. Those pundits, too, were taking the least charitable view of the event.

Few pundits of any persuasion attempt to be charitable. Instead, they play this game of "Gotcha." The net result for most people is that reading their favorite pundits actually reduces and narrows their understanding of issues.

Consider three goals that a political pundit might have. One goal might be to open the minds of people on the other side. Another goal might be to open the minds of people on the pundit's own side. A third goal might be to close the minds of people on the pundit's own side. Nearly all the punditry that appears in the various media today serves only the third goal. The pundits act as if what they fear most is that their followers will be open to alternative points of view. To me, these media personalities appear to be fighting a constant battle to keep their followers' minds closed. The saddest part is that I believe they are succeeding. Political polarization has risen.[10]

Let me hasten to point out that I do not classify myself as a centrist. I am not looking for some sort of "Kumbaya" compromise that tries to satisfy everyone. I believe that on any given issue, libertarianism usually gets you to the best answer. However, the point of the three-axes model is to give people a tool for communication, not to steer the outcome of that communication in my direction.

The use of the three-axes model is analogous to the use of personality-type indicators by organizations. Experts in organizational behavior believe that some of the friction that often builds among people in an organization results from personality differences. Many training programs are based on the idea that increased knowledge of personality psychology can enable employees in an organization to better understand one another and to benefit from the strengths that people with different personalities bring to the enterprise.

The first personality test widely used in business was the Myers-Briggs Type Indicator. That test remains very popular, even though many academic psychologists prefer something known as OCEAN, or the five-factor model.

Before I elaborate on the analogy between understanding other political languages and understanding other personality types, let me emphasize that I am *not* trying to explain differences in political beliefs as a function of personality type or psychological makeup. That may be an interesting project, but I want to stay away from it. I want to encourage taking everyone's political opinions at face value, rather than demeaning others by saying that "You believe X because you have personality type Y." Reductionism, or taking other people's opinions at less than face value, is suited to closing minds on one's own side, which is the opposite of my goal here.

With the three-axes model, I am not trying to help you explain away the political beliefs of those with whom you disagree. On the contrary, I am proposing a framework that provides insight into the different languages spoken by people of various political ideologies. I believe in trying to understand the other person's language, as opposed to trying to psychoanalyze why he or she speaks it.

When businesses use Myers-Briggs, their goal is to enable people to detach from their preferred style of thinking to better communicate with and manage people with different styles. For example, some people are inclined to think in big-picture terms, whereas others are inclined to think in details. Absent any training, the big-picture person thinks that the detail-oriented person is small-minded. The detail-oriented person sees the big-picture person as careless. Each thinks that the other is stupid. However, in many situations it is necessary to combine both outlooks. Successful organizations are able to integrate people who focus on the big picture with people who are concerned with details. Understanding your Myers-Briggs type in relation to other types can enable you to respect, to communicate with, and to manage people with personalities different from your own.

Another Myers-Briggs axis is known as "judging versus perceiving," with the former preferring to see issues as closed and the latter more comfortable treating issues as open. A "judging" manager is inclined to drive team meetings toward conclusions, checking off decisions before others can process and accept them. A "perceiving" manager is inclined to let meeting participants ruminate longer and is even willing to reopen questions that appear to have been decided earlier. In the absence of Myers-Briggs training, a meeting run by a judging type will drive a perceiving type nuts, and vice versa. With the training, each type of person can more easily detach from his or her own point of view, to appreciate the merits of the other's style and to communicate with the other type of person more effectively. That is what I want the three-axes model to achieve in political discussions.

It is possible, I suppose, that the best way for people of differing ideological heuristics to get along is to avoid one another.

A 2012 Pew Research study found that 18 percent of social networking site users had "unfriended" someone because of political postings, most often because of disagreement.[11] In 2004, journalist Bill Bishop coined the term "big sort" to describe the phenomenon in the United States of people becoming more clustered among those with similar political views. Four years later, along with sociologist Robert Cushing, Bishop published a book on the topic. According to the authors' analysis, the red counties in America are getting redder and the blue counties are getting bluer.

Taken to its limit, sorting ourselves by political ideology would break up the United States. There would be a progressive country, a conservative country, and a (small) libertarian country. However, the process of getting from here to there would be quite difficult, to say the least. In a divorce, how would the assets and liabilities of the dis-United States be divided up? What court system would have jurisdiction regarding disputes between citizens of conservative America and progressive America?

For me, a politically segregated America would be dystopian, if it were even feasible. I like most of the people with whom I disagree. If anything, I have more close friends among people who differ from me politically than among those who share my political outlook.

Another fantasy is to cause the demise of other ideologies by eliminating their voices in education and the media. If you are a progressive with such a fantasy, you want to get rid of Fox News, talk radio, right-wing think tanks, and advertising funded by corporations and wealthy conservatives. If you are a conservative, you want to get rid of "tenured radicals" on college campuses, "political correctness" in public schools, and the "mainstream media." For their part, libertarians for decades have been seeking to "educate" Americans, particularly in economics. Bryan Caplan, a libertarian economist who wrote the 2007 book *The Myth of the Rational Voter: Why Democracies Choose Bad Policies*, believes that more economic education leads to more libertarian views.

What I am suggesting here is that we treat differing ideologies as if they were languages to be understood rather than heresies to be stamped out. Perhaps your ultimate goal is to win people over to your ideology. But to use an oft-quoted phrase from Stephen Covey's best-selling 1989 book *The 7 Habits of Highly Effective People*, "Seek first to understand, then to be understood."

In fact, I do not think one's goal should be to win everyone over to the same ideology. I think one's goal for others should be that they have open minds. And if that is my goal for others, then it should also be the goal that I set for myself.

5

Your Mind on Politics: Motivated Reasoning

In late September of 2018, Americans were riveted by the spectacle of Supreme Court nominee Brett Kavanaugh facing an accusation that he committed sexual assault as a teenager. People who followed the drama formed strong opinions regarding his guilt or innocence. What is striking is that those opinions were almost perfectly correlated with people's political inclinations regarding the desirability of appointing a conservative to the court.

Everyone could see the same evidence, which was inconclusive if one took a detached perspective. Progressives emphasized that his accuser, Christine Blasey Ford, recalled Kavanaugh as the perpetrator of a traumatic assault. Conservatives emphasized that the other people that she named as present at the home where the assault took place had no memory of the incident. This difference in emphasis is best explained by a phenomenon known as motivated reasoning.

If people were open-minded, you would think that the more information they had, the more they would tend to come to agreement on issues. Surprisingly, political scientists and psychologists have found the opposite. More polarization exists among well-informed voters than among poorly informed voters. Moreover, when you give politically engaged voters on opposite sides an identical piece of new information, each side comes away believing more strongly in its original point of view. Political psychologists have coined the term "motivated reasoning" to describe this phenomenon.

When we engage in motivated reasoning, we are like lawyers arguing a case. We muster evidence to justify or reinforce our preconceived opinions. We embrace new facts or opinions that support our views, while we carefully scrutinize and dispute any evidence that appears contradictory.

With motivated reasoning, when we explain phenomena, we focus on what we *want* the cause to be. The philosopher Robert Nozick jokingly referred to this as "normative sociology."[12] For example, what accounts for the high incarceration rates of young African American males? A progressive would look to racism in our justice system and society as the cause.

A conservative would look to high crime rates as the cause. And a libertarian would look to drug laws as the cause.

In his book *Thinking, Fast and Slow*, psychologist Daniel Kahneman describes two ways that humans process information. One way is a fast process that is intuitive and instinctive, and the other is a slow process that is more deliberate and careful. He calls the former System 1 and the latter System 2. One might use System 2 when making a more thoughtful decision. However, Kahneman emphasizes that often we engage System 2 not to make a decision but instead to rationalize a conclusion reached by System 1. In political thinking, System 2 may be engaged in motivated reasoning.

Conceptually, I like to think of dividing System 2 into two components, a lawyer and a judge. The lawyer component engages in motivated reasoning, protecting our existing beliefs. When it encounters other points of view, it homes in on their weakest arguments, attacking them viciously and uncharitably. It overlooks similar weaknesses in our own arguments.

The judge component engages in deliberative reasoning. It tries to truly understand other points of view. It does not evaluate either side more charitably than the other. It does not overlook the strengths in other people's points of view or the weaknesses in our point of view.

I hope to encourage open-minded political reasoning, whereby we attempt to think like an impartial judge rather than an aggressive lawyer. With open-minded reasoning, you would apply an equal standard of rigor to evidence that supports or contradicts your previous views. With open-minded reasoning, you are open to changing your views, or at least to acknowledging that your views are not the absolute truth.

6

Further Thoughts on Human Nature

My observations concerning the three-axes model have led me to think about human nature, which I view as the product of our biological and cultural evolution. Why have we evolved to rely so much on motivated reasoning, and why is our political speech rarely open-minded? Why do we have separate political tribes in the first place? Why do we have the tribes of progressivism, conservatism, and libertarianism?

You should treat my thoughts on human nature as highly speculative. They are based in part on my interpretation of the work of various scholars, but those scholars should not be blamed for any errors in my views.

Using a computer analogy, I think of humans as having biological hardware, an operating system given by evolution, and cultural applications. When it comes to eating, our hardware handles digestion, our operating system tells us when we are hungry and inclines us toward sugary and fatty foods, and our culture shapes the food that is available and attractive to us.

Our biological hardware gives us some basic capabilities and constraints. Our operating system—meaning the capabilities and inclinations that we acquired during the long period when human society consisted of small bands of hunter-gatherers— gives us strong tendencies. Our cultural software consists of the norms and habits that we have developed over the years. Our hardware and the operating system are given. But our cultural applications can evolve rapidly and can sometimes overcome inclinations that come from the operating system.

One component of our operating system is that group membership is important. As a hunter-gatherer, if you were tossed out of your group and left on your own, you probably became miserable and soon died. It is still very important to us to feel accepted by a group.

Other components of our operating system lead us to formulate and enforce norms against cheaters. For example, it is in the interest of an individual to steal food from others in a group. However, if everyone thinks it is easier to steal food than to work for it, then no one will work for food and the group will starve. Our ancestors who survived had operating systems that inclined us to punish thieves. More generally, our operating system gives us an instinct to obey social norms and to encourage others to obey social norms.

As Adam Smith pointed out, we have a desire for high self-regard. In part, we want to be recognized by others as being admirable. Moreover, each of us has what Smith called an "impartial spectator," or conscience, which makes us feel happier when we believe that we are acting in a way that others will regard highly. Following group norms is a way to please the impartial spectator.

We have an instinct to recognize and reward cooperators, meaning people who obey social norms even when it is not in their immediate interest to do so. We have an instinct to punish defectors, meaning people who opportunistically violate social norms.

Another component of group-oriented hardware is our desire for prestige in a group. We value prestige, we compete for prestige, we admire prestigious individuals, and we seek to imitate those people. For example, in academia, markers of prestige include academic rank, such as adjunct professor, assistant professor, associate professor, full professor, or chaired professor. In addition, academics pay attention to departmental and institutional rankings. Competition is keen to obtain positions that have high prestige.

In contrast, we resent dominance, in which powerful individuals attempt to rule over others using intimidation. In small bands of apes, when one ape becomes too dominant, other apes will form coalitions to defeat the alpha ape.[13]

Groups must balance the need to enforce norms with the need to adapt. If the group is unable to enforce social norms, then there will be too much cheating, and cooperation will break down. However, if the group is too rigid in its social norms and forbids experimentation, then it will fail to adapt to new circumstances.

Groups must also balance competition with cooperation. When there is no external threat to the group, competition inside the group can be healthy. However, when there is an external threat, then a group needs to summon the ability to cooperate. Peter Turchin, a scholar who studies historical cultural dynamics, has argued that groups on a border between two large ethnic populations tend to be particularly threatened and, if such groups survive, they tend to have acquired enough cooperative norms to be able to expand into empires. For example, Turchin argues that American settlers and aboriginal Native Americans threatened one another and that to win this contest, the settlers had to overcome internal differences, such as cultural differences between English settlers of New England and German settlers of Pennsylvania.

Although our desire to please the impartial spectator can lead us to obey social norms, psychologist Jonathan Haidt suggests that we also can improve our self-regard by rationalizing our behavior when we violate social norms. In *The Righteous Mind: Why Good People Are Divided by Politics and Religion*, he argues that moral reasoning evolved originally to enable us to justify our actions to others. In my terms, Haidt is saying that moral reasoning evolved as motivated reasoning rather than as open-minded reasoning.

For example, in today's fast-food restaurants, we have cultural software that tells us that we should clear the table and throw out our trash when we finish eating. We do not want others to frown on us, so we follow this norm. Even if no one else is watching, our self-regard is higher if we follow the norm. However, someone who does not follow the norm might engage in rationalization. ("My toddler was crying, and I was in a hurry to take her out of there.")

Because we value being accepted by a group, we cooperate and sacrifice for the good of a group with whom we feel close. We have much less natural willingness to sacrifice in order to help distant strangers.

In addition, we care about the status of our group or tribe relative to that of other tribes. Successful tribes are ones in which status in the tribe depends in part on demonstration of tribal loyalty. A tribe will expect you to demonstrate loyalty by participating in unpleasant rituals and by making sacrifices for the benefit of a tribe. A tribe will punish disloyal members with banishment. It will reward loyal members with higher status.

One reads of hunter-gatherer tribes in which coming of age requires engaging in some act of war against a rival tribe. In most modern organizations, you do not have to kill or injure an opponent to achieve status. However, many of the other methods of demonstrating tribal loyalty are still very much present: rituals, linguistic differences, requirements to affirm group beliefs, and so on. One of the ways to affirm group beliefs is to participate in the verbal denunciation of other groups.

Because displays of loyalty can enhance one's status in a tribe, we can expect individuals to attempt to "cheat" or to "game the system" by appearing to make sacrifices and to participate in unpleasant rituals without actually doing so. As economist Robin Hanson has observed, we can expect human nature to include a large measure of hypocrisy.[14] By the same token, humans have developed an ability to detect and punish cheaters, free riders, and hypocrites.

It is in this context of tribal gamesmanship that linguistic differences emerge. People use such differences to enhance tribal cohesion and to sharpen contrasts with other tribes.

Linguistic differences persist because one tribe often wants another tribe *not* to understand what is being said. Think of American football, where a quarterback will change a play at the last minute by calling an "audible." He shouts a few codes with the intention of enabling his teammates to coordinate while keeping their plans secret from the opposing team.

I doubt that language evolved in order to be universally understood. Instead, I believe that language evolved to be understood by some people and not understood by others. (I have not seen this hypothesis articulated elsewhere. Take it as speculation on my part.) Although political speech is not as consciously coded as a football "audible," it often serves a similar purpose: to align one tribe while mystifying another.

If we have evolved to seek status in a tribal context, then it is easy to see how motivated reasoning in politics would emerge. We can demonstrate loyalty to our tribe by arguing in support of our group's beliefs and attacking the beliefs of rival groups. The more skilled we become at doing so, the higher our status will be in the group.

Conversely, open-minded reasoning may not be so well rewarded. If you find merits in the other group's point of view, you risk losing status to those who are more unambiguously loyal. If you go too far, you may be branded a traitor and shunned by your tribe.

The theory that tribes seek differentiation in language, rituals, and beliefs may explain the phenomenon of disagreement. In their paper "Are Disagreements Honest?," economists Tyler Cowen and Robin Hanson suggest that the existence of persistent disagreement is evidence that people are not rational truth seekers.[15] Cowen and Hanson propose that people have self-serving beliefs and deceive themselves. In my terminology, people engage in motivated reasoning at an unconscious level but believe consciously that they are engaged in open-minded reasoning.

My explanation for persistent disagreement is to interpret "self-serving beliefs" as beliefs that enhance one's status in a tribe. Of course, expressing beliefs that elevate the status of my tribe relative to that of rival tribes can be particularly effective for raising my status in my tribe.

Thus, I would view political disagreement as a *social* phenomenon rather than an individual one. We naturally tend to organize into tribe-like groups. Tribes differentiate in part on the basis of shared beliefs, including political beliefs. Our inclination to seek high status in a tribe leads us to become loyal to the beliefs of our tribe. This results in persistent disagreement.

Why do we not coalesce into one big political tribe? Or, conversely, why do we not have more, smaller political tribes?

One possible answer is that political tribes fit different personality types. If there are a few personality types that differ from one another, then this might explain political tribal alignments. But I am reluctant to make too much of the purported link between personality and political beliefs. Instead, it seems to me that we select our political tribes on the basis of socialization rather than fit with our personalities. For example, I doubt that the fact that some demographic groups vote heavily Democratic while others vote heavily Republican can be traced to voters' psychological tendencies as measured by, say, the five-factor model.

Another possibility is that people have a desire to affiliate with a large group that is viewed as having a high moral purpose. Such an idea has been proposed as an explanation for loyalty to a nation-state by Robert Nisbet in *The Quest for Community* and by Daniel Klein in "The People's Romance."[16]

Moreover, the sense of moral purpose is strengthened if the group can be distinguished from other groups. That is, the significance of our moral purpose is higher if our group has an enemy.

For many centuries, major religions met people's desire to belong to a large group with a higher moral purpose. Many people attached great significance to their religious affiliation. They went to war over differences in religious faith.

Psychology professor Jordan Peterson has written the following:

> In a sophisticated religious system, there is a positive and negative polarity. Ideologies simplify that polarity and, in doing so, demonize and oversimplify.[17]

I believe that it is not a coincidence that as religious sentiment has weakened, political sentiment has strengthened. There remains an instinct to divide the world between a highly principled "we" and an amoral "they," and political beliefs can serve that purpose. Moreover, just as people used to be able to quickly identify coreligionists by their use of distinctive expressions associated with a particular faith, I think that people today can quickly identify political allies by listening for arguments that employ their preferred axis.

If I may be allowed to speculate further, I would suggest that the individual axes I have identified happen to have strong emotional appeal. They speak to deep concerns. They may not be embedded in our operating systems, but they have deep roots in our cultural software.

For example, the oppressor-oppressed axis is an essential element in the biblical tale of the Exodus, one of the most well-known and powerful stories ever written. The oppressive Egyptian pharaoh is one of history's most infamous villains, and Moses, the leader of the oppressed Hebrew slaves, is one of its most famous heroes. And I would note that American Jews often can be found among the progressives who respond to the oppressor-oppressed axis. I would note also that Karl Marx tapped into the oppressor-oppressed axis, with his depiction of the capitalist class and the proletariat.

My claim is that the enduring power of the Exodus story is a sign that our cultural software includes a strong resonance with the oppressor-oppressed axis. The story would not have achieved such a central place in Western culture if people were indifferent to oppression.

The civilization-barbarism axis also is deep-seated. Peter Turchin points out that in times of war, each side thinks that it is fighting against a barbaric race. With history written by the winners, we think of the Romans as representing civilization in their conflicts with outsiders. However, with a little reflection on Romans' conduct (slavery, deadly gladiatorial combat), we can see that the case that they represented moral virtue against barbaric opponents is not so clear-cut.

Returning to the present, as Americans we may have no doubt that suicide bombing is a barbarous tactic but that aerial drone strikes are legitimate. However, in countries where drone strikes have killed innocent civilians, the outlook might be different.

My reading of Turchin is that under conditions of war, an advantage accrues to groups that are able to demonize their enemies as barbaric, because such a belief strengthens the fighting spirit of the group's soldiers. Part of the cultural software that promotes group survival is a willingness to do whatever it takes to win a war. Cultures that survived are cultures that could fight more cohesively. They were aided by a belief that they were defending civilization against barbarism. Our cultural ancestors were sensitive to the civilization vs. barbarism axis, and we have inherited some of their sensitivity.

Jordan Peterson, in his YouTube lectures,[18] suggests that many ancient myths include a sequence of events in which a good king dies, a bad king inherits the throne and becomes a tyrant, and the bad king's tyrannical rule results in chaos. A new hero rises to fight the forces of chaos, and the new hero becomes a good king. The hero in these myths must overcome all three of my negative polarities: oppression, barbarism, and coercive tyranny.

The cultural software that aligns with the liberty-coercion axis may not be as easily located in ancient stories, but one can find recent examples. These examples include the stories of the American Revolution (Patrick Henry's famous words, "Give me liberty or give me death!"), Mark Twain's *The Adventures of Huckleberry Finn*, and George Orwell's *1984*.

Again, the ideas in this section are highly speculative, and the errors contained here do not necessarily invalidate the three-axes model. That said, this section can be summarized as follows:

People need to affiliate with groups. Moreover, as we settled into larger groups than hunter-gatherer bands, we evolved a need to belong to groups that embody a higher moral purpose. For centuries, major religions met this need, but now the need is being met increasingly by political affiliation.

When it comes to affiliating with groups that embody a higher moral purpose, we do not naturally fragment into small groups or coalesce into a single group. Instead, we seem to have a tendency to divide into large tribes.

Each of the axes in the three-axes model resonates with our cultural software. However, somehow the groups into which we have fallen in our political affiliations differ in terms of which axis clearly represents the concerns of each particular group.

7

The State of Closure: Discrediting the Opponent

NFC [need for closure] refers to an aversion toward ambiguity and uncertainty, and the desire for a firm answer to a question. When NFC becomes overwhelming, *any* answer, even a wrong one, is preferable to remaining in a state of confusion and doubt.

—Dylan Evans[19]

I believe that we often use political reasoning to arrive at a state of *closure*. This state is one in which we have eliminated any doubt about our beliefs that might otherwise arise when we encounter people whose beliefs are different. When our tribe has a stance on an issue and some fact or analysis threatens to undermine that belief, this creates cognitive dissonance. Getting rid of that dissonance becomes a priority. We summon our reasoning to fend off the threatening information in much the same way that a homeowner might summon the police to fend off an intruder. An important part of the process of attaining closure is demonstrating the disreputable nature of those supplying the threatening information.

Motivated reasoning is part of this process of obtaining closure. For example, suppose that a study comes out suggesting that tax cuts do not help grow the economy. Your eagerness to find methodological flaws in the study is likely to differ on the basis of your previous inclinations. On the one hand, if you were already inclined, because of your tribal affiliation, to believe that tax cuts *do* help the economy grow, then you would focus intently on finding methodological flaws in the new study. On the other hand, if you were convinced before that tax cuts do not help the economy to grow, then you would be inclined to praise the study without examining its methodology.

Another step in attaining closure is explaining away the beliefs of those with whom we disagree. In fact, we go so far as to believe that we understand our opponents better than they understand themselves. Why doesn't Jack share Jill's views? If you ask Jill, she will say that she knows the "real Jack." She understands Jack better than he understands himself. The way Jill sees it, if Jack knew what she knew, he would come around to her point of view.

David McRaney, author of the blog *You Are Not So Smart*, describes this as the "illusion of asymmetric insight." Describing a series of experiments conducted in 2001 by researchers Emily Pronin, Lee Ross, Justin Kruger, and Kenneth Savitsky, McRaney writes the following:

> The results showed liberals believed they knew more about conservatives than conservatives knew about liberals. The conservatives believed they knew more about liberals than liberals knew about conservatives. Both groups thought they knew more about their opponents than their opponents knew about themselves.[20]

(Note that the illusion of asymmetric insight would suggest that I know less than I believe I know about the views of those with whom I disagree, which in my case would mean progressives and conservatives. Readers should bear that in mind.)

Overall, to arrive at a state of closure on an issue, you will do as follows:

- Come to a position on the issue that will be welcomed by the other members of your tribe.

- Consider yourself able to refute any arguments made against this position.

- Be able to account for contrary beliefs held by others. This ability means you will use asymmetric insights that account for why other people are unable to recognize that they are wrong.

My claim about the three-axes model is that one's dominant heuristic plays an important role in this process of closure, particularly at the third step. As a progressive, you have achieved closure when you have become convinced that those with whom you disagree are at best indifferent to the suffering of the oppressed. As a conservative, you have achieved closure when you have become convinced that those with whom you disagree are at best indifferent to the phenomenon of people losing their respect for civilized values and institutions and reverting to barbarism. As a libertarian, you have achieved closure when you have become convinced that those with whom you disagree are at best indifferent to the expansion of government's scope and power.

If you are a progressive, you may find yourself saying that what conservatives and libertarians really want is a hierarchical society where the rich can exploit the poor at will. As a conservative, you may find yourself saying that what progressives and libertarians really want is to tear down all of society's civilizing institutions. As a libertarian, you may find yourself saying that all progressives and conservatives want is a freedom-smothering nanny state. Attributing bad motives to other tribes is part of this drive for closure.

8

The Ideological Turing Test

Economist Bryan Caplan coined the term "ideological Turing test" to denote a thought experiment in which you are placed in a room with a group of people holding a different ideology and your task is to pretend to share their ideology. If they are convinced that you are one of them, then you have passed the test.

To pass the ideological Turing test, you would have to genuinely understand an ideology with which you do not agree. Instead, as we saw in the previous chapter, we tend to *presume* that we understand people with differing ideologies *better* than they understand themselves. Person A thinks about person B, "I know what you *really* believe." However, from B's perspective, A holds a straw-man view.

For example, in his 2012 book *Libertarianism: What Everyone Needs to Know*, Jason Brennan writes:

> American politics has two large camps. The first camp advocates an American police state—one that polices the world at large while policing its citizens' lifestyles. It advocates having government promote traditional Judeo-Christian virtues. It wants to marginalize or expel alternative modes of life. The second camp advocates an American nanny state—one that tries to nudge and control the behavior of its citizens "for their own good." Both camps support having the government manage, control, and prop up industry and commerce. In rhetoric, a vicious divide separates the two camps. Yet when in power, the two camps act much the same.[21]

That characterization of progressives and conservatives would not pass an ideological Turing test. If you walk into a room of conservatives and advocate an American police state, the conservatives will not embrace you. In ordinary language, a police state means a state in which ordinary people live in constant fear of armed forces that exercise arbitrary and unlimited power.

Similarly, if you walk into a room of progressives and advocate an American nanny state, the progressives will not embrace you. In ordinary language, a nanny state means a state perceived as having excessive control over the welfare of its citizens, such as the mental institution in Ken Kesey's 1963 book *One Flew Over the Cuckoo's Nest*. In that institution, the staff employs rules and manipulative techniques that are supposedly in the best interest of the patients but which deprive those patients of freedom and dignity. Such a state is so compulsive in its effort to shield us from the consequences of our weaknesses that we lose our individual agency.

As much as we may not like the restrictions that conservatives wish to impose on others, it is an overstatement to claim that those restrictions would amount to a police state. As much as we may not like the approaches progressives wish to take to try to help people they see as disadvantaged, it is an overstatement to claim that those policies would amount to a nanny state. To say that those dystopias are what conservatives and progressives *advocate* is to put up straw men.

These straw men are equivalent to a false argument that says, "Libertarians want to see poor people starve." You are welcome to argue that libertarian policies would cause poor people to starve. However, if you say that you advocate having people starve, libertarians will not embrace you as one of their own. You will not pass an ideological Turing test.

I believe that using the three-axes model could help one to pass an ideological Turing test. That is, if you are with a group of progressives and you frame an issue in terms of the oppressor-oppressed axis, then you will be viewed as an ideological soulmate. (Note, however, that the oppressed groups must belong to generally accepted social classes viewed as oppressed. Do not attempt to smuggle in "conservatives" as an oppressed group.) This also works if you are with a group of conservatives and you frame an issue in terms of the civilization-barbarism axis, or if you are with a group of libertarians and you frame an issue in terms of the liberty-coercion axis.

However, to truly pass the ideological Turing test, you would have to be aware of other dispositions that differ among progressives, conservatives, and libertarians. I believe that one can discern differences in attitudes toward human nature, history, science, technology, and markets.

Progressives believe in human *betterment*. They see nearly unlimited potential for humans to improve materially and, more important, morally.

Conservatives believe in human *weakness*. In biblical terms, man is "fallen." The dark side of human nature will never be eradicated. It can be tamed only by social institutions, including the family, religion, and government. Take away those institutions, and what emerges is a situation similar to what is described in William Golding's 1954 novel, *Lord of the Flies*.

Libertarians believe in human *rationality*. People pursue ends, and they act as they do for good reasons.

Progressives are inclined to revere *science*. They believe that science can help in the project of human betterment. They put social science on par with physical science, and they embrace social science as a guide to public policy. They believe that they must protect science from conservatives who disdain it.

Conservatives are inclined to revere the *past*, including religious tradition. Conservatives tend to be less optimistic than progressives and libertarians about the future. Conservatives fear that civilization is or will soon be in decline, because of a loss of traditional values.

Libertarians are inclined to revere *technology*. Whether it is Ayn Rand writing of industrialists or modern libertarians extolling Bitcoin, libertarians see technology as a liberating force. Libertarians are less likely than progressives or conservatives to be concerned with the adverse effects of technology.

Progressives view markets as *unfair*. Progressive economists focus on what are termed "market failures," which they believe can and must be addressed by using government policy. Even more troubling in their view is that success in the market often reflects luck, and it may be an unjust reward for exploitation.

Conservatives view markets as promoting *virtue*. Success in the market must be earned and is usually well deserved.

Libertarians view markets as promoting *peaceful cooperation*. Everyone succeeds in the market, because each voluntary exchange benefits both parties, and the entire network of voluntary exchange creates prosperity.

In short, there is more to the differences among progressives, conservatives, and libertarians than the moral frames along the three axes. But if one is going to pass an ideological Turing test, it is particularly important to understand those moral frames.

9

I'm *Reasonable,*
They're *Not*

Who among us has not thought the following?

> I cannot be pigeonholed on the basis of heuristics.
> I arrive at my political beliefs through careful reason-
> ing and consideration of the evidence. It is a charac-
> teristic of those who share my political beliefs that we
> carefully weigh the facts and arrive at realistic, sound
> conclusions. It a characteristic of those on the other
> side that they are slaves to dogma and impaired in
> their use of reason.

Just as each of us believes in our own free will, each of
us believes that we are open-minded whereas others are
unreasonable. Concluding that others are unreasonable is a

necessary step in the process of arriving at closure, as described earlier.

One of my prescriptions for slow political thinking is to try to avoid telling yourself, "*I'm* reasonable, *they're* not." Instead, I would suggest the following rule of thumb.

The only person you are qualified to pronounce unreasonable is yourself.

You are qualified to tell other people that they are *wrong*. You are just not qualified to tell other people that they are *unreasonable*. Only they can be the judge of that. In fact, one corollary of the rule of thumb is that when you find yourself pronouncing those with whom you disagree as unreasonable, that would be a good time to be concerned about your own reasonableness. Rather than pronounce others as unreasonable, I recommend just focusing on explaining where they are wrong. If by some chance they pronounce themselves unreasonable, then fine. But you are not qualified to do so.

On rare occasions, individuals discover that they have been unreasonable. For example, I have taught economics at a high school where athletes are sometimes dismissed early to go to games. One day, I came to class with materials to hand out for a project, and four students had already left without telling me or making any arrangements with me in advance. I was angry, and I sent them an email telling them that their grade for the quarter was going to be reduced by five points.

The students were in the wrong. It is customary at the school for students to notify teachers at least a day in advance of planned absences. And it is a rule that they must arrange to make up work. However, I had not established ahead of time any penalty. So I came to the conclusion that I had been unreasonable and I rescinded the email. I will concede that such events are rare, but they do indicate that people are capable of pronouncing themselves unreasonable.

Pronouncing *others* unreasonable, in contrast, helps us achieve closure, but it does not help those people. I would say that if you are lucky, sometimes you can convince others that they are wrong. They may go on to conclude that their previous beliefs were not reasonable. But pounding the table and asserting that someone else is being unreasonable adds nothing to your argument.

10

Using All Three Languages: Examples

One benefit of being able to understand all three languages of politics is that it becomes easier to recognize the reasonableness of the positions held by others. Those positions still may seem wrong, but it will be possible to understand where other people are coming from.

For example, consider immigration policy. Like many libertarians, I am in favor of open borders. From the liberty-coercion perspective, an open border gives the individual a choice about government. The more that people are denied that choice, the worse off they are. Consider North Korea, for example, where citizens are essentially prisoners of the regime.

In the case of the United States, I would like to see anyone be allowed to work here and to apply for citizenship. I see the employment relationship as a voluntary agreement that benefits both parties. I do not believe that one's ability to live and work in the United States should be impaired because you happen to have been born somewhere else.

Obviously, not everybody sees it that way. To a conservative, opening the U.S. border would invite our culture to be buried underneath a sea of alien values. It would be an open invitation to terrorists and to other barbarian threats. National boundaries are an integral part of the traditional order, say the conservatives, and the potential for disorder from tearing them down seems alarming.

To a progressive, the idea of aiding people who are oppressed in other countries has appeal. However, the United States already has an asylum program that is intended to accomplish that. Progressives worry that allowing more people to work here will drive down wages, adversely affecting an important oppressed group—namely, low-skilled working people. Those of us on the open-borders side of the issue would argue that protecting American low-skilled workers makes life worse for the low-skilled workers who are not allowed to immigrate, but this argument does not really compute along the oppressor-oppressed axis.

Although I think that conservatives and progressives are both wrong on the issue, I think they are being reasonable. Given their respective concerns, their positions make sense.

Consider another difficult issue, that of determining the cause of the mortgage meltdown that produced the financial crisis of 2008. Each heuristic can provide a plausible explanation.

Progressives assign much of the blame to banks exploiting weak individuals, which aligns with the oppressor-oppressed heuristic. There is certainly something to this. Financial institutions are more sophisticated than individuals. Many of the mortgages that borrowers took on were loans with adjustable rates that would have made them very expensive. Nevertheless, there are some problems with this narrative. Many of the borrowers began to miss payments well before the interest rates adjusted. Many of the loans that defaulted were for non-owner-occupied homes, indicating that borrowers were engaged in speculation. Finally, the financial cost of default was borne much more by investors than by borrowers. Because many of the loans were made with little or no down payment, the borrower could abandon the home with only a relatively small financial loss. Investors lost hundreds of billions of dollars because they were left holding properties that were worth far less than the value of the mortgages.

Had the financial institutions been swindling the home-owners, the results would have been profits at the banks at the expense of individuals. That was not the case. It is true that some lenders were able to profit from originating bad loans and pawning them off to various institutional investors, including the government-sponsored enterprises Freddie Mac and Fannie Mae. However, that is a case of sophisticated financiers gaining at the expense of other sophisticated financiers, not at the expense of ordinary individuals.

Whereas conservatives would not go so far as to say that generous lending standards were barbaric, they still would view the episode in terms of the civilization-barbarism axis. That is, traditional lending was based on sound values that made funds available only to those borrowers who met certain conditions. Borrowers needed to have appropriate ethics related to work and thrift, along with the willingness to defer gratification to come up with a sizable down payment. As with any departure from tradition, lending to borrowers who lacked those traits was a dangerous endeavor.

Conservatives often blame the debacle on goals set by the government for low-income and minority borrowers. According to this view, major lending institutions, including

Freddie Mac, Fannie Mae, and large commercial banks, had to seek unqualified borrowers to satisfy government quotas. To do so, those institutions had to lower their standards for down payments, documentation requirements, and credit history. This story is plausible in principle because lending standards certainly plummeted during the housing bubble. Some studies lend support to the thesis that the government's lending quotas were a factor. However, other studies suggest little or no effect from the quotas. Many of the riskiest loans were originated by firms that were not subject to this form of regulatory pressure (although one could argue that these firms were counting on regulated firms maintaining a market for these loans).

Libertarians also look at government as the ultimate source of the problem. Libertarian economics is closely aligned with the Austrian school, and Austrian economists view central banks as the Dennis the Menace of capital markets, distorting interest rates and causing bubbles. Again, there is some plausibility to this, because housing prices did experience a bubble. However, there are problems with blaming this on Fed interest-rate policy, because it is difficult to explain the evolution of the interest rate controlled by the Fed (the Fed funds rate), mortgage rates, and house prices. From January of 2002 through January of 2009, as the Fed moved its rate up and down, the mortgage rate remained relatively stable, between 5.25 percent and 6.75 percent. The most spectacular phase of the house price bubble was 2005–2006, and it is hard to see how this was connected to mortgage rates, which drifted toward the high end of their range in those two years.

Other libertarians, including me, have focused on the perverse impact of bank capital regulations. In what ultimately proved to be a misguided attempt at sophisticated control over bank activity, agencies in the most advanced countries collaborated on a set of risk-based capital requirements, known as the Basel Accords. The goal of international collaboration was to avoid a race to the bottom in regulation and instead to ensure that banks in all countries faced similar rules. Because bank safety and soundness is such an important regulatory goal, the Basel Accords set strict standards that required banks to maintain more capital against assets deemed to be risky than against assets deemed to have less risk. Unfortunately, in 2001, the assets designated as low risk were expanded to include mortgage securities with AAA ratings from the major bond-rating agencies. In hindsight, this expansion proved to be quite a blunder.

In my opinion, these explanations for the mortgage meltdown are not equally persuasive. As indicated, I lean toward the last of these. However, the point I wish to stress is that all the explanations are reasonable. Nobody is relying on heuristics in the face of contrary evidence that is overwhelming, undeniable, and determinative. In that sense, I think it would be wrong to accuse someone of being an ideologue for holding a particular point of view.

Nonetheless, the explanations that people put forth for the mortgage meltdown tend to be highly correlated with their dominant heuristic in politics. To some extent, everyone is a bit of an ideologue. I have seen many "research" papers that provide analysis that is consistent with how I would have expected the author to conclude, on the basis of his or her previous political propensities. I have not seen any that fail to do so.

One conclusion that I draw from this example is that no one seems to be able to be objective when analyzing the mortgage meltdown. An implication is that it is very unlikely that *I* am the one who is objective and that those who disagree with me are unreasonable. And yet my sense of myself is that I *am* objective. It is very difficult to reconcile logic and intuition in this regard.

Philosophers refer to this as the problem of naïve realism, meaning that each of us naïvely believes that our perspective is real, even though different perspectives contradict one another. Psychology professor Matthew D. Lieberman explains the consequences of naïve realism.

> If I am seeing reality for what it is and you see it differently, then one of us has a broken reality detector and I know mine isn't broken. If you can't see reality as it is, or worse yet, can see it but refuse to acknowledge it, then you must be crazy, stupid, biased, lazy or deceitful.

> In the absence of a thorough appreciation for how our brain ensures that we will end up as naïve realists, we can't help but see complex social events differently from one another, with each of us denigrating the other for failing to see what is so obviously true.[22]

To protect our naïve realism, our natural inclination is to engage in motivated reasoning. That is, we are disposed to treat facts and analysis as credible when they speak the language of our dominant heuristic, while we seek reasons to dispute or dismiss facts and analysis that speak a different language.

If we want to shift from motivated reasoning and instead attempt to de-center and to be objective, then we have to resist the inclination to give critical scrutiny only to facts and analysis that threaten our beliefs. We should give some benefit of the doubt to contrary evidence. Moreover, we should be as eager to poke holes in analysis that speaks to our dominant heuristic as we are to poke holes in contrary analysis.

For example, suppose that you are a libertarian and that someone reports on a study showing that choice and competition improve primary education. Your inclination, before you even see how the study was conducted, is to praise the study, because it aligns with your emphasis on the liberty-coercion axis. Instead, I recommend that you analyze the study as if it had reached the opposite conclusion. Imagine that the findings were that choice and competition make primary education worse, and with that mindset scrutinize the study for methodological weaknesses.

11

Donald Trump and the
Three-Axes Model

Donald Trump shook up the political landscape. In hindsight, one can say that he capitalized on a public mood of suspicion toward established elites and what is called the "liberal international order."

In his important book *The Revolt of the Public*, Martin Gurri points out that the latest communications media have empowered new popular movements everywhere, from the Arab Spring to Brexit. Gurri paints a picture of a nihilistic public, offended by what they see as a corrupt and inept ruling class.

It is well to recall that in the United States, the electorate has long had an ornery streak. Voters frequently hop on bandwagons to support relatively inexperienced presidential candidates running against Washington veterans: Jimmy Carter vs. Gerald Ford in 1976, Ronald Reagan vs. Carter in 1980, Bill Clinton vs. George H. W. Bush in 1992, Barack Obama's primary challenge against Hillary Clinton in 2008, and Obama vs. John McCain in 2008.

In only one presidential election in my lifetime has a candidate with considerable Washington experience defeated an outsider. That was in 1988, when the elder Bush trounced former Massachusetts governor Michael Dukakis.

One can see Trump's defeat of Clinton as more typical of the pattern in which voters prefer political innocence to experience. It seems that a significant segment of the American public views Washington as corrupt and alien. Clinton's experience may well have been a handicap. Many Americans instead are enamored of the ideal of the amateur citizen-crusader.

Yet Trump was an extreme case. Unlike any previous successful outsider candidate, he gained almost no endorsements from major party figures in his campaign for the Republican presidential nomination. And unlike Obama, for example, Trump had to fight through mostly negative media coverage.

To the extent that one can find a coherent theme to the public's revolt that brought Trump to Washington, it would appear to be one of trying to minimize America's exposure to globalization. In the 2017 edition of this book, and drawing on David Brooks's *Bobos in Paradise: The New Upper Class and How They Got There*, I suggested that Trump mobilized voters who were anti-Bobo. The Bobos are the cosmopolitan "bourgeois bohemians," Brooks's term for the contemporary American elite, who seem more at home in Prague than in Peoria.

In his book, published in 2000, Brooks illustrated elite taste by listing some prominent individuals whom he believed the Bobos regarded as insufficiently intellectual to merit respect. First among those was Donald Trump. Today, many Bobos despise Trump and his supporters, and the feeling is mutual.

A cosmopolitan vs. nationalist conflict has emerged in other countries as well. Italians elected a government consisting of two parties that disagree on virtually everything other than opposition to the cosmopolitan elite. Nationalist, anti-elite sentiment also has found expression in elections in the United Kingdom, Germany, France, and Eastern Europe.

Thus, the triumph of Donald Trump probably should not be viewed as a victory for purely traditional conservatism. Instead, the Trump coalition added some anti-cosmopolitan swing votes to those of traditional conservatives, even as the candidate alienated a few of the more cosmopolitan conservatives.

During the election campaign, Trump made little or no use of the rhetoric of the civilization vs. barbarism axis that I claim galvanizes conservatives. In fact, many of the best-known conservative writers, such as George Will and Jonah Goldberg, were vehemently opposed to Trump. They were put off by his disrespect for the Republican Party leaders, for civil discourse, and for key conservative principles such as free trade.

The conservative intellectual leaders who could not abide Trump probably were a sliver of the overall population. Conservatives in the electorate at large tended to support Trump, in some cases with enthusiasm and in other cases because they saw him as the lesser of two evils. As an example of the latter, Michael Anton published under a pseudonym an essay called "The Flight 93 Election," in which he alleged that "a Hillary presidency will be pedal-to-the-metal on the entire Progressive-left agenda, plus items few of us have yet imagined in our darkest moments."[23]

Since taking office, President Trump has on a few occasions rung the civilization-barbarism bell. In July of 2017, he gave a speech in Warsaw, Poland, in which he said,

> Polish heroes and American patriots fought side by side in our War of Independence and in many wars that followed. Our soldiers still serve together today

in Afghanistan and Iraq, combatting the enemies of all civilization. . . .

We urge Russia to cease its destabilizing activities in Ukraine and elsewhere, and its support for hostile regimes—including Syria and Iran—and to instead join the community of responsible nations in our fight against common enemies and in defense of civilization itself. . . .

We write symphonies. We pursue innovation. We celebrate our ancient heroes, embrace our timeless traditions and customs, and always seek to explore and discover brand-new frontiers.

We reward brilliance. We strive for excellence, and cherish inspiring works of art that honor God. We treasure the rule of law and protect the right to free speech and free expression.

We empower women as pillars of our society and of our success. We put faith and family, not government and bureaucracy, at the center of our lives. . . .

What we have, what we inherited from our—and you know this better than anybody, and you see it today with this incredible group of people—what we've inherited from our ancestors has never existed to this extent before. And if we fail to preserve it, it will never, ever exist again. So we cannot fail.[24]

The response to this speech was what the three-axes model would predict. Conservatives lauded the speech as a statement of American values.[25] Progressives interpreted it in terms of the oppressor-oppressed axis as carrying a subliminal message of racism.[26] Libertarians found fault with Trump's hostility toward immigration and free trade.[27]

In August and September of 2018, President Trump's nomination of Brett Kavanaugh to the Supreme Court provoked responses that again fit with the three-axes model. When the nominee was accused of having engaged in improper sexual conduct in the past, progressives focused on the victim status of women. Conservatives focused on what they saw as the violation of norms on the part of Democratic senators and some journalists in the manner in which they promoted allegations. Some libertarians took the view that Kavanaugh deserved the rights of an accused person to insist that allegations be accompanied by proof in order to be credible.

But I would suggest that Trump defines his supporters less as conservatives than as allies in his personal battles with major media outlets and with the probe by the special counsel into his campaign. These supporters see him as besieged by "fake news" and the "deep state." As of this writing, they remain staunchly in the corner of their anti-Bobo champion.

The issue of cosmopolitanism vs. nationalism has given us a new axis. Trump has found a new enemy to rally against. Where progressives rally against oppressors, conservatives rally against the forces of barbarism, and libertarians rally against state coercion, Trump's supporters rally against cosmopolitanism. The tribal psychology is that of the three-axes model, but there is a different axis.

The net result is to make "talking across the political divides" even more difficult today than it was when I wrote the previous editions of this book. The ideologies of progressivism, conservatism, and libertarianism each have an intellectual tradition behind them. The three axes arc just simple heuristics or demonization tactics used by people who fall within those traditions. But literature is available for those who want to find the best arguments for alternative points of view and to explore their nuances.

The populist-nationalist movement does not have a similar background of intellectual ferment and development. Anti-Boboism is pretty much tribalism stripped to its essence, without a well-articulated set of governing principles or policy goals.

For the most part, Trump's opponents do not wish to issue a stout defense of cosmopolitanism. Instead, they denounce Trump's supporters as racists and xenophobes. Progressives prefer to mobilize against their traditional demons: the oppressor class. This language does not speak to the anti-Bobos any better than it speaks to conservatives or to libertarians.

In fact, "tribalism stripped to its essence" seems to describe all segments of American politics in the Trump era. Progressives are too offended by Trump to countenance any effort to reach out to conservatives. Instead, they seem to be drifting further away from the center. This makes it easy for Republicans to rationalize sticking together as a tribe, as they did during the Kavanaugh confirmation battle.

There is a segment of the public that is weary of political tribalism, and I see myself as belonging to that segment. But some structural features of American politics work against us. Cultural sorting and political gerrymandering have created many Congressional districts in which the winner is determined in a party primary as opposed to a general election. In such districts, centrist candidates are at a disadvantage. Presidential primaries, too, tend to pull candidates toward partisan extremes.

The media environment is one of desperate competition for audience share. In this context, the most sensationalist, outrage-stimulating coverage is most effective. It seems the typical news consumer is sufficiently partisan to be inclined to click away from any attempt to provide a charitable or nuanced depiction of the other side.

The news cycle is very short, with yesterday's big story forgotten by tomorrow. It is sad to note that the stories with the longest shelf life are not about international conflict or government spending priorities. Instead, they tend to be stories like the "migrant caravan" of asylum seekers from Central America. The stories that get the most coverage are those that activate people along their various axes: oppressor-oppressed, civilization-barbarism, liberty-coercion, and cosmopolitan-nationalist.

I hope that people will develop immune responses to the media outrage-feeding machine. I hope that the next surprise political bandwagon forms behind a candidate who practices civility. In short, I hope that the increase in the use of languages of demonization that has taken place since I first wrote this book will be reversed shortly after the Trump era ends.

Conclusion

I have proposed a model in which contemporary Americans who are politically engaged take differing positions on complex issues. Most of us are committed members of one of the major political tribes, which I call progressive, conservative, and libertarian. We are concerned about our status in our tribe, and each tribe confers higher status on members who extol its virtues and condemn the vices of other tribes.

For praise and condemnation, each tribe prefers a different language. For a progressive, the highest virtue is to be on the side of the oppressed, and the worst sin is to be aligned with the oppressor. For a conservative, the highest virtue is to be on the side of civilizing institutions, and the worst sin is to be aligned with those who would tear down those institutions and thereby promote barbarism. For a libertarian, the highest virtue is to be on the side of individual choice, and the worst sin is to be aligned with expanding the scope of government.

I have proposed a conceptual distinction between fast political thinking and slow political thinking. I believe that complex issues demand slow political thinking. Instead, the three languages of politics play a prominent role in motivated reasoning, which narrows our minds, producing friction, anger, and frustration with those with whom we disagree. The three languages let us reach closure too readily, so that we lose sight of the ambiguity that is often present in difficult political issues.

We can reason more constructively by remaining aware of the languages of politics. Being aware of your own language can allow you to recognize when you are likely to be overly generous in granting credence to those who provide arguments expressed in that language. Being aware of other languages can give you better insight into how issues might appear to those with whom you disagree.

Thinking of political differences as differences in language can help to reduce frustration. However, the language metaphor goes only so far. With language, there is hope that you can translate what you want to say in your language into the language that someone else understands. Unfortunately, there is no one-for-one translation that takes you from a given political language to another.

I believe that most difficult political issues are sufficiently complex that they cannot be understood fully using just one heuristic. If that is the case, then we probably will be much wiser if we can detach ourselves from our preferred language. In addition, treating people who use other heuristics as reasonable is likely to prove a less stressful and more productive way of approaching politics than treating the other heuristics as heresies that must be stamped out.

Afterword

My original intuition, back in 2013, was that most political commentary was intended not to persuade but to reinforce. People of one political viewpoint speak in a language that resonates only with those who share that viewpoint.

In recent years, observers have increasingly taken note of the tribalism in politics that the three-axes model exemplifies. This afterword collects some of the analyses by pundits and political scientists that have appeared in recent years and that discussed this tribalism.

In September 2017, columnist Andrew Sullivan wrote an essay in which he pondered whether American democracy can survive.[28]

> Over the past couple of decades in America, the enduring, complicated divides of ideology, geography,

party, class, religion, and race have mutated into something deeper, simpler to map, and therefore much more ominous. I don't just mean the rise of political polarization (although that's how it often expresses itself), nor the rise of political violence (the domestic terrorism of the late 1960s and '70s was far worse), nor even this country's ancient black-white racial conflict (though its potency endures).

I mean a new and compounding combination of all these differences into two coherent tribes, eerily balanced in political power, fighting not just to advance their own side but to provoke, condemn, and defeat the other. . . .

One tribe lives on the coasts and in the cities and the other is scattered across a rural and exurban expanse; where one tribe holds on to traditional faith and the other is increasingly contemptuous of religion altogether; where one is viscerally nationalist and the other's outlook is increasingly global; where each dominates a major political party; and, most dangerously, where both are growing in intensity as they move further apart.

Sullivan goes on to write,

> Tribalism, it's always worth remembering, is not one aspect of human experience. It's the default human experience. It comes more naturally to us than any other way of life. For the overwhelming majority of our time on this planet, the tribe was the only form of human society. We lived for tens of thousands of years in compact, largely egalitarian groups of around 50 people or more, connected to each other by genetics and language, usually unwritten. Most tribes occupied their own familiar territory, with widespread sharing of food and no private property. A tribe had its own leaders and a myth of its own history. It sorted out what we did every day, what we thought every hour. . . .

> After a while, your immersion in tribal loyalty makes the activities of another tribe not just alien but close to incomprehensible. It has been noticed, for example, that primitive tribes can sometimes call their members simply "people" while describing others as some kind of alien.

Incidentally, Sullivan's essay was illustrated beautifully by a drawing of three groups of sheep. Sheep in each group were huddled together as closely as possible; as a result, the groups were completely separate from one another.

In November 2017, psychology professor Jonathan Haidt gave a lecture titled "The Age of Outrage."[29] He said:

> When we look back at the ways our ancestors lived, there's no getting around it: we are tribal primates. We are exquisitely designed and adapted by evolution for life in small societies with intense, animistic religion and violent intergroup conflict over territory. We love tribal living so much that we invented sports, fraternities, street gangs, fan clubs, and tattoos. Tribalism is in our hearts and minds. We'll never stamp it out entirely, but we can minimize its effects because we are a behaviorally flexible species.

Haidt pointed out the following:

> Data from Gallup and Pew show steadily rising polarization since the 1990s, whether you ask people how much they dislike the other side, how much they think the other side is a threat to the country, or how upset they'd be if their child married someone from the other side.

To me, media competition helps explain why the story of professional football players kneeling during the national anthem managed to outlast many other controversies in the fast-paced news cycle. Conservatives were outraged by the protests, because the national anthem is a symbol of our civilization. Progressives were outraged by those who condemn the kneeling football players, because progressives see the protesters as fighting for the oppressed. Libertarians were outraged by the sacred status given to the ritual of saluting the flag, which is a symbol of state power.

Related to the topic of tribal solidarity, philosophy professor C. Thi Nguyen wrote an essay in which he distinguished between not listening to the other side and not trusting the other side.[30] Nguyen argued that political tribes are like cults, in that members face strong social pressure to trust only their fellow partisans and to distrust people on the other side.

Political scientist Lilliana Mason studied political polarization for her PhD dissertation, which she adapted as a book, *Uncivil Agreement: How Politics Became Our Identity*. By "identity," Mason means your propensity to call yourself a conservative or a liberal or a Republican or a Democrat. The more strongly you identify with your political tribe, the more favorably you are likely to view other members of that tribe and the more unfavorably you are likely to view members of the opposite tribe. Strength of political identity is measured by the positive feelings you have toward supporters of your political party and even more by the negative feelings you have toward opponents.

Mason's research concerns the relationship between strength of political identity and opinions on issues. It turns out, for example, that identity shapes opinions more than the other way around. Mason writes:

> More often than not, citizens do not choose which party to support based on policy opinion; they alter their policy opinion according to which party they support . . . citizens want to believe that their political values are solid and well reasoned. More often, though, policy attitudes grow out of group-based defense. Partisanship muddies the folk pathway from interests to outcomes, sometimes sending a person in a wrong direction or further down a path than self-interest and values alone would dictate.[31]

Along these lines, in his essay "America Wasn't Built for Humans," Andrew Sullivan had noted that

> When a party leader in a liberal democracy proposes a shift in direction, there is usually an internal debate.

It can go on for years. When a tribal leader does so, the tribe immediately jumps on command. And so the Republicans went from free trade to protectionism, and from internationalism to nationalism, almost overnight.[32]

Mason found that the increase in political polarization in recent decades reflects a strengthening of political identity more than an increased division on issues. Policy disagreements have not become much sharper. But "American partisans have become more biased, intolerant, angry, and politically active than their policy disagreements can explain."[33]

To explain this, Mason refers to some classic experiments in social psychology in which people are assigned to arbitrary teams and given a game to play or a task to perform. Participants develop positive attitudes about their teammates and negative attitudes about members of the other team.

Mason hypothesizes that political identity has strengthened because of demographic sorting. Political affiliation has become more highly correlated with other elements of identity, including social class, education, occupation, and religious outlook. With fewer "cross-cutting identities," people have less direct contact with those who disagree on political issues. This increases the "other-ness" of people who do not share our political affiliation and makes us less likely to attribute positive human qualities to them.

One of Mason's points is that political emotions can become stronger without positions on issues becoming more polarized. Political scientists Marc Hetherington and Jonathan Weiler describe polling trends in their 2018 book *Prius or Pickup?: How the Answers to Four Simple Questions Explain America's Great Divide*. In particular, they examine a "feeling thermometer," in which they characterize a temperature of 20 degrees or less as hate.

> The percentage of partisans who really seem to hate the other party has skyrocketed since the turn of the millennium. . . . From 1980 through 2000, the number of partisans who rated their feelings about the opposing party as 20 degrees or less never exceeded twenty percentage points, and was usually much lower. After 2000, however, the percentage of partisans with hatred in their hearts rose with each election: from the 20s and 30s for Democrats and Republicans in 2008, to 48 and 50 percent, respectively, in 2016.[34]

In his 2018 book *Them: Why We Hate Each Other—and How to Heal*,[35] Sen. Ben Sasse (R-NE) connects political polarization to personal loneliness and a decline in community involvement. He suggests that closer local community connections would be an antidote to political tribalism:

> Humans are social, relational beings. We want and need to be in tribes. In our time, however, all of the traditional tribes that have sustained humans for millennia are simultaneously in collapse. Family, enduring friendship, meaningful shared work, local communities of worship—all have grown ever thinner. We are creating thicker, more vehement tribes around our political differences, I believe, because there is a growing vacuum at the heart of our shared (or increasingly, not so shared) everyday lives.[36]

All these recent efforts show that I am not alone in identifying the increase in tribal hostility as a problem in contemporary political life. Although previous editions of *The Three Languages of Politics* did not succeed in stemming this tide, it is encouraging that more observers are now concerned with the issue.

Appendix: Testing the Three-Axes Model

The three-axes model might be tested in a number of ways. One approach would be to create a survey using three-axes formulations and use the survey to see how well it distinguishes among self-described progressives, self-described conservatives, and self-described libertarians.

Another approach, suggested by Tyler Cowen, would be to undertake a content analysis of leading columnists of the various genres. Ideally, I think that one person would select the columnists and classify their ideologies. A random selection of columns would be stripped of information that would give away the identity of the columnist and given to someone else familiar with the three-axes model. That person would mark all passages that pertain to the three axes.

Then we would see how well the columnists align with the three-axes model.

I attempted a less ambitious effort along those lines. In late January 2013, I examined then-recent columns available on the internet from E. J. Dionne (a progressive), Victor Davis Hanson (a conservative), and Nick Gillespie (a libertarian). Note that, as conducted entirely by me, this sort of exercise is rich with potential for confirmation bias. Note also that the most prominent recent news event had been the Newtown, Connecticut, school shooting (also referred to as Sandy Hook), so columns were skewed toward the issue of gun control.

My analysis supported the model. For each columnist, I found numerous instances that used the expected axis. Use of other axes was less frequent, typically sarcastic, and never with enthusiasm. Following are the results for each columnist. (All columns are from 2013, except as noted.)

E. J. Dionne's Columns

I reviewed the following columns by the progressive, E. J. Dionne:

"Reagan Is Obama's Touchstone" (January 24, 2013, http://www.arcamax.com/politics/ejdionnejr/s-1268382)

"The Liberation of Barack Obama" (January 21, 2013, http://www.arcamax.com/politics/ejdionnejr/s-1265992)

"Obama Takes On Extremism on Guns" (January 16, 2013, https://www.washingtonpost.com/opinions/obama -takes-on-extremism-on-guns/2013/01/16/25a8b778 -601d-11e2-9940-6fc488f3fecd_story.html?)

"We're Not in Decline or Retreat" (January 14, 2013, http://www.arcamax.com/politics/ejdionnejr/s-1262445)

"Gun Sanity Needs Bipartisanship" (January 10, 2013, https://www.realclearpolitics.com/articles/2013/01/10 /gun_sanity_needs_bipartisanship_116634.html)

I found the following excerpts that pertain to the oppressor-oppressed axis:

Indeed, his [President Obama's] very identity— yes, as a black man, but also as someone who is urban, highly educated and culturally progressive— sometimes served to aggravate the divides in our body politic: between the North and the South, the rural and the metropolitan, the young and the old, the liberal and the conservative, the traditional and the modernist. And racism always lurked, barely below the surface, as another force pulling us apart.

The president is now free to address the needs of the poor as well as those of the middle class. He can answer the aspirations of working people battered by economic change without fearing that promoting fairness could crater the financial system by disaffecting investors. He can set about proving that a decent level of economic security and social justice can actually foster entrepreneurial dynamism, risk-taking and inventiveness.

. . . the lobbies that purport to speak for gun owners (while actually representing the interests of gun manufacturers) don't care what the public thinks.

. . . he sought to mobilize a new effort to counteract the entrenched power of those who have dictated submissiveness in the face of bloodshed.

Consider that until so many children were gunned down, the National Rifle Association and the gun manufacturers for which it speaks were able to block calls for a legislative response in the wake of one massacre after another.

The following excerpt showed an awareness of the civilization-barbarism axis, but with half-hearted concern:

> Yet Obama and Vice President Joe Biden also worked hard to find middle ground in their anti-violence program in drawing on concerns raised since the Sandy Hook tragedy by gun rights advocates. Obama thus addressed not only firearms issues but also the imperative to improve school security and our mental health system, as well as the need to know more about the impact of violent video games.

I found nothing in Dionne's columns that pertained to the liberty-coercion axis.

Victor Davis Hanson's Columns

I reviewed the following columns by the conservative, Victor Davis Hanson:

"Europe's Wishes Came True" (January 24, 2013, http://townhall.com/columnists/victordavishanson/2013/01/24/europes-wishes-came-true-n1495817)

"The War Between the Amendments" (January 17, 2013, http://townhall.com/columnists/victordavishanson/2013/01/17/the-war-between-the-amendments-n1490541)

"When Big Deficits Became Good" (January 10, 2013, http://townhall.com/columnists/victordavishanson/2013/01/10/when-big-deficits-became-good-n1485482)

"2012: When Dreams Died" (December 27, 2012, http://townhall.com/columnists/victordavishanson/2012/12/27/2012-when-dreams-died-n1474172)

"The New Racial Derangement Syndrome" (December 20, 2012, http://townhall.com/columnists/victordavishanson/2012/12/20/the-new-racial-derangement-syndrome-n1470329)

Along the axis of civilization-barbarism, I found the following:

> Neither the EU at large nor most individual European nations can sustain their present rate of redistributionist entitlements. To end cash transfers across borders spells the breakup of the union. To embrace austerity at home ensures near anarchy in the streets of individual nations.

> Muammar Gadhafi's dictatorship was replaced with chaos that has birthed a terrorist haven that threatens to become the new Afghanistan. The odious anti-Semite

and Muslim Brotherhood leader Mohamed Morsi now runs a near-bankrupt Egypt that looks a lot like Haiti. After the messes in Libya and Egypt, the West watched impotently as Syria became something like Mogadishu.

In Algeria, radical Islamists brazenly executed dozens of Western hostages.

The Hawaiian-born and Indonesia-raised president certainly seems more interested in Asia than he does in the old colonial Mediterranean world of aging and shrinking European nations, Arab quagmires, oil intrigue, Islamic terrorists and the Israeli-Palestinian open sore.

Like a knife or bomb, a gun is a tool, and the human who misuses it is the only guilty party. An armed school guard might do more to stop a mass shooting on campus than a law outlawing the shooter's preferred weapon or magazine.

Homeowners should have the right to own weapons comparable to those of criminals, who often pack illicit semi-automatic handguns.

Just as semi-automatic weapons mark a technological sea change from the flintlock muskets of the Founders' era, computer-simulated video dismemberment is a world away from the spirited political pamphleteering of the 18th century. If we talk of restricting the Second Amendment to protect us against modern technological breakthroughs, why not curtail the First Amendment as well?

How about an executive order to Hollywood to stop its graphic depictions of mass killings, perhaps limiting the nature and rationing the number of shootings that can appear in any one film? Can't we ban violent video games altogether in the same way we forbid child pornography? Isn't it past time for an executive order to curtail some of the rights of the mentally unstable—given that the gunmen in mass killings usually have a history of psychic disorders and often use mood-altering drugs?

The growth of entitlements is popular with many voters, especially given that 47 percent pay no federal income taxes.

So far, the fantasy of jailing a single Coptic filmmaker for posting an anti-Islamic video has trumped the reality of holding the administration accountable for allowing lax security and offering only feeble responses to a massacre prompted by a planned, al Qaeda–affiliated terrorist attack on a U.S. diplomatic post.

Steps toward a far more realistic solution—jawbone Hollywood to quit romanticizing gratuitous cruelty and violence; censor sick, macabre video games; restrict some freedoms of the mentally ill; and put armed security guards into the schools—are as much an anathema to civil libertarians as the banning of some guns is a panacea. So we pontificate while waiting for the next massacre.

Given the chaos of Libya and Syria, and the murder of Americans in Benghazi, the cruel winter of 2012 has now ended the dreamy Arab Spring of 2011.

. . . there are ominous signs of impending financial implosion at home. Abroad, we see a soon-to-be nuclear Iran, an even more unhinged nuclear North Korea, a new Islamic coalition against Israel, a bleeding European Union, and a more nationalist Germany and Japan determined to achieve security apart from the old but increasingly suspect U.S. guarantees.

. . . are we returning to the racial labyrinth of the 19th-century Old Confederacy, where we measure our supposed racial DNA to the nth degree?

For nearly a half-century, cultural relativism in the universities taught that racist speech was only bigotry if it came from those—mostly white—with power. Supposedly oppressed minorities could not themselves be real racists. But even if that bankrupt theory was once considered gospel, it is no longer convincing—given that offenders such as actor and musician Jamie Foxx, comedian Chris Rock, and Rev. Joseph Lowery (who was given the Presidential Medal of Freedom by Obama) are among the more affluent and acclaimed Americans. [Note the sarcastic treatment of the oppressor-oppressed axis.]

Stirring up the pot for short-term political gain in a multiracial society is abjectly insane. If the new racialism grows unchecked, it will eventually lead to cycles of backlash and counter-backlash—and some day to something like the Balkans or Rwanda.

People are just people. But they can turn into veritable monsters when—as a great American once warned—they look to the color of our skin rather than the content of our character.

Along the liberty-coercion axis, I found the following:

. . . the chief purpose of the Second Amendment was not necessarily just to ensure personal protection from criminals or the freedom to hunt with firearms, but in fact to guarantee that a well-armed populace might enjoy some parity to an all-powerful, centralized government. To the Founders, the notion that individual citizens had recourse to weapons comparable to those of federal authorities was a strong deterrent to government infringing upon constitutionally protected freedoms—rights that cannot simply be hacked away by presidential executive orders.

That may be why the brief Second Amendment explicitly cites the desirability of a militia. By intent, it was followed by the Third Amendment, which restricts the rights of an abusive government to quarter federal troops in citizens' homes.

Along the oppressor-oppressed axis, I found another example that, in context, was sarcastic:

> Higher taxes, weighted heavily toward the affluent, spread the wealth and correct the inequities of market-based compensation.

Nick Gillespie's Columns

I reviewed the following columns from the libertarian, Nick Gillespie:

"Barack Obama, Jon Stewart, Sandy Hook, and 'Common Sense' Gun Control" (January 15, 2013, http://reason.com /archives/2013/01/15/jon-stewart-sandy-hook)

"Examine Inequality's Causes Before Prescribing Solutions" (December 30, 2012, http://reason.com/archives /2012/12/30/examine-inequalitys-causes-before-prescr)

"4 Awful Reactions to Sandy Hook School Shooting— and Thoughts on a Better Response" (December 15, 2012, http://reason.com/archives/2012/12/15/4-archetypally -awful-reactions-to-sandy)

"Please Read This If You Think Deficits Don't Matter and That Spending Doesn't Drive Deficits." (December 1,

2012, http://reason.com/archives/2012/12/01/if-you-dont
-think-spending-is-at-the-roo)

"Why Mitt Romney Lost—and the GOP Will Continue to Lose" (November 9, 2012, http://reason.com
/archives/2012/11/09/why-mitt-romney-lost-and-the-gop
-will-co)

Along the liberty-coercion axis, I found the following:

Cue more nutjobs and numbskulls—such as
conspiracy-monger Alex Jones—talking about how
guns are the last line of defense against tyranny.
[Gillespie was talking about Jon Stewart's satirical
take on gun rights advocates.]

The notion that a rag-tag band of regular folks armed
with semi-automatic weapons and the odd shotgun
are a serious hedge against tyranny strikes me as a
stretch. . . .

Hitler and the Nazis didn't take away everyone's
guns, as is commonly argued. They expanded gun
rights for many groups (though not the Jews).

[Note: In the foregoing quotes, the libertarian columnist is expressing skepticism toward one of the

liberty-coercion arguments used in the gun control debate.]

And yet the idea of armed self-defense is a totally different matter and I also realize that many people live out in the sticks or even in urban neighborhoods where the police aren't a realistic option when trouble comes a-calling. I know people for whom owning a shotgun is no different than owning a tennis racket and hunting is a family affair more revered than holiday dinners. I don't see any reason why law-abiding people should have to explain to anyone why they want a semi-automatic gun or a magazine that holds 10 bullets instead of seven.

It's probably always been the case but certainly since the start of 21st century, it seems like we legislate only by crisis-mongering and the results have not been good: The PATRIOT Act, the Iraq War, TARP, fiscal cliff deals, you name it. Would that cooler heads prevailed then and now.

Are you going to start making "strange" kids go to more psychological clinics at earlier ages? Lock up more psychos (and define that term more broadly) and/or take them away from parents? Institute a house-by-house search for insane people in proximity to guns? Ban or limit video games that generate billions of dollars in sales and essentially zero in copycat crimes?

. . . there's still 26 people—kids mostly, which is just awful—who had no connection to the gunman who shot them down. And taking a couple of bullets out of clip or sending more kids to doctors or turning schools slightly more into prison environments isn't going to bring them back.

In what some have seen as an echo of the setting for *The Hunger Games*, the growing power of the federal government to dispense favors and direct whole industries has transformed the Washington, D.C., metro area into the nation's wealthiest, boasting 10 of the top 20 counties for median household income.

. . . even the most vociferous proponents of locking up potential killers grant that maybe 10 percent of schizophrenics become violent. Academic studies of presumptive detention of the mentally ill suggest that mental health professionals do about as well, and sometimes worse, than regular people in figuring out who exactly is going to go postal. Such results should temper any and all calls to start rounding up more people in the name of protecting innocents.

Many of the same people who are now calling for immediate action with regard to gun control recognize that The Patriot Act, rushed through Congress in the immediate aftermath of the 9/11 attacks, was a terrible piece of legislation that ultimately did nothing to protect Americans even as it vastly expanded the state's ability to surveil law-abiding citizens. There's no reason to think that federal, state, or local gun control laws promulgated now would result in anything different.

All to pay for, what, military adventures that have done precious little to reduce the world's supply of suffering? Or for expanded drug benefits for already-wealthy seniors? For a war against weed that has turned the Home of the Free into history's greatest jailer nation?

. . . on broadly defined social issues such as immigration, marriage equality, and drug policy, Barack Obama has been terrible. He's deported record numbers of immigrants and his late-campaign exemption of some younger undocumented immigrants was one of the most cynical policy changes imaginable. Yet he managed to increase his takc of the Latino vote precisely because Mitt Romney and the Republicans are even worse (at least rhetorically) on the issue. Romney called for "self-deportation" during the Republican primary season and attacked Gov. Rick Perry—who pulls upward of 40 percent of Latino voters in Texas—for his mildly pro-immigrant stance (in his 2004 re-election bid, George W. Bush received around 40 percent on the Latino vote). If Republican representatives such as Steve King (R-Iowa) continue to talk about immigrants as akin to dogs and livestock, there's no way that the party can expect Hispanics to vote for them. Or non-Hispanics who are rightly disturbed by such attitudes.

Obama has raided medical marijuana dispensaries that are legal under state law without a second thought. Now that Washington and Colorado have legalized not just medical marijuana but all pot, the GOP should stay true to its valorization of federalism and the states as "laboratories of democracy" and call for an end to the federal drug war. The same goes for gay marriage, which is supported by a majority of Americans and passed in Maryland, Maine, and Washington state—even as an anti–marriage equality amendment to Minnesota's state constitution went down to defeat. It's fully consistent for small-government Republicans—who rarely miss an opportunity to talk about returning "power" to the states—to champion these developments.

There's no question that the media and Democrats made a huge deal out of Todd Akin's bizarre biological disquisitions and Richard Mourdock's principled commitment to an extreme pro-life position. But the reason such statements resonated with voters is because they confirm the idea of the GOP as an anti-sex, anti-abortion party that routinely says the government is awful at everything it does but should have the final say over whether women can get abortions. George W. Bush and a Republican Congress (whose leadership remains firmly in power) massively expanded state spending and control of all aspects of life.

To the extent that the GOP offers a choice on broadly defined social issues, it is a party anchored firmly in the past that needs the federal government (of all entities) to enforce its desired positions on abortion, drug legalization, and marriage.

The following showed awareness of the civilization-barbarism axis, but Gillespie is trying to rebut it:

According to data compiled by the National Center for Education Statistics, schools have been getting safer and less violent at least over the past couple of decades—despite what (former Arkansas Governor Mike) Huckabee would doubtless consider a period of rising godlessness. During the school year of 1992–93, for instance, the number of on-location murders of students and staff at K–12 public schools was 47 (out of population of millions). In 2009–2010 (the latest year for which data is listed), the number was 25. Over the same period, the rate on victimizations per 1,000 students for theft dropped from 101 to 18. For violent crimes, the rate dropped from 53 to 14. And for "serious violent" crimes, the rate dropped from 8 to 4.

Further Reading

I have taken the approach in the main text of keeping references to the literature of psychology and politics to a minimum. Here, I want to describe some of the works that have influenced me the most.

1. George Lakoff, *Moral Politics: How Liberals and Conservatives Think* (Chicago: University of Chicago Press, 2002). A version has been available on the internet since 1995, and it can still be found at http://www.wwcd.org/issues/Lakoff.html.

Lakoff suggests that liberals speak the language of "nurturant parent morality" and conservatives speak the language of "strict father morality."

The nurturant parent believes that every child is inherently good and needs only guidance and nurturing from parents. The strict father believes that every child is inherently wicked and needs strict authority to stay on the straight and narrow.

Lakoff says that most people view government through the lens of their preferred parental metaphor. Thus, nurturant parents want government to provide guidance and nurturing. Strict fathers want government to focus on order and discipline.

Lakoff does not seem to distinguish between the political masses and the politically engaged elite. I consider that distinction to be important. Whereas Lakoff may be correct in his intuition about how the political masses process political rhetoric, I think his model works less well for those who are highly engaged politically. I think that someone using this model would badly fail an ideological Turing test, especially among conservatives. Indeed, Lakoff is a committed progressive, and an important part of his agenda is to tune progressive rhetoric to win electoral contests with conservatives.

I believe that progressives have a more romantic vision of government than the nurturant parent metaphor captures. That metaphor does not speak to the pain of the oppressed, the evil of oppression, or the nobility of government when it serves the cause of justice.

I believe that conservatives have a broader view of the problem of barbarism than is represented by the strict-father model. Few conservatives see their own children as wicked. However, they do see wickedness in the world, and they see traditional institutions as necessary in order to preserve and protect civilization.

Finally, libertarians would reject as totally inappropriate the analogy between government and family. I can only imagine a libertarian mocking Lakoff: "If A and B are both adults, does A become B's parent by virtue of winning an election? Do your parents threaten to put you in prison if you do not pay taxes to them?" And so on.

2. Thomas Sowell, *A Conflict of Visions: Ideological Origins of Political Struggles* (New York: Basic Books, 2002).

Sowell comes from the opposite end of the political spectrum from Lakoff. Sowell's thesis is that progressives have an *unconstrained* vision, whereas conservatives hold a *constrained* vision.

The unconstrained vision is that those in the progressive camp have sufficient wisdom and knowledge to carry out policies that would lead to great human betterment. On the other side are those who profit from the status quo or who are blinded by prejudice and misinformation. If the opposition can be overcome, a glorious vision can be realized.

The constrained vision is that humans are not capable of gaining perfection. Moreover, those who would implement schemes for betterment are themselves afflicted with human character flaws. Furthermore, they lack the necessary wisdom and knowledge to prescribe choices for others. From this conservative perspective on the limits of human potential, the progressive project can only end in tragedy.

The conservative view is that social problems reflect constraints. The progressive view is that social problems reflect the failure of good to overcome evil in the political sphere.

Another aspect of the unconstrained vision is that a person exists whom Sowell calls a "surrogate decision-maker." That is, there is an expert, willingly chosen by the people, who can make the right choices. Conservatives do not believe that such an expert exists. I would say that libertarians are even more adamant on this point. For libertarians, people are experts at making their own choices and bumbling fools when making choices for others.

3. Jonathan Haidt, *The Righteous Mind: Why Good People Are Divided by Politics and Religion* (New York: Pantheon, 2012).

Whereas Lakoff, Sowell, and I arrive at our theories of political beliefs by introspection, Haidt uses psychological instruments, notably surveys, to refine his theories.

Haidt believes that people consider a limited set of factors when making moral judgments. He argues that liberals and conservatives differ in the weights that they give to these factors.

Haidt's factors are like axes, with the first word the positive end of the axis and the second word the negative end of the axis. The axes are as follow:

- care/harm
- fairness/cheating
- liberty/oppression
- loyalty/betrayal
- authority/subversion
- sanctity/degradation

Haidt's claim is that progressives focus most on the first three, whereas conservatives put some weight on all six. Libertarians put an especially heavy weight on liberty/oppression.

I am skeptical of these axes. For example, I suspect that the weight that one gives to, say, loyalty/betrayal depends on the institution that is specified in the question. Progressives may be less concerned about loyalty to America the country, but they could be just as concerned about tribal loyalty to the worldwide progressive cause. They may be less concerned about sanctity relative to traditional religious values, but they could be just as concerned about sanctity relative to ecology and diet. And so on.

I am strongly inclined to go along with Haidt in his views on human nature. He makes a good case for suggesting that, starting from a violent, status-fixated chimpanzee mentality, we gradually learned to collaborate, and as a result we evolved *some* moral intuitions that incline us to cooperate and to punish defectors.

I also take from Haidt the view that moral reasoning is often rationalization, or what I have been calling (and what others have called) motivated reasoning. Haidt's model appears to be that our morality comes from intuition, with reason serving as our defense lawyer. I depart from this model by positing a capacity for constructive reasoning. This capacity may or may not be something that psychologists can locate in the brain, but I find it much more comfortable believing that constructive reasoning exists, so that I do not have to view all reasoning as motivated reasoning.

4. Daniel Kahneman, *Thinking, Fast and Slow* (New York: Farrar, Straus, and Giroux, 2011).

Kahneman is another empirically oriented psychologist. He provides the easy-to-grasp model of humans as having System 1, which is quick and intuitive, and System 2, which is slow and considered. It is easy to translate Haidt's model into these terms. Haidt would say that our moral positions are driven by System 1, and System 2 is then tasked with explaining and defending those positions. As noted earlier, I prefer to believe (hope?) that it is possible for System 2 to operate as a judge, not just as a lawyer.

5. Drew Westen, Pavel S. Blagov, Keith Harenski, Clint Kilts, and Stephan Hamann, "Neural Bases of Motivated Reasoning: An fMRI Study of Emotional Constraints on Partisan Political Judgment in the 2004 U.S. Presidential Election," *Journal of Cognitive Neuroscience* 18, no. 11 (2006): 1947–58, http:// www.datascienceassn.org/sites/default/files/Neural%20 Bases%20of%20Motivated%20Reasoning%20-%20An%20 fMRI%20Study%20of%20Emotional%20Constraints% 20on%20Partisan%20Political%20Judgment%20in%20 the%202004%20U.S.%20Presidential%20Election.pdf.

I believe that this study is one of the most important studies of motivated reasoning. The neuroscience is over my head, so to speak. But here are a couple of excerpts:

> Consistent with prior studies of partisan biases and motivated reasoning, when confronted with information about their candidate that would logically lead

them to an emotionally aversive conclusion, partisans arrived at an alternative conclusion. This process was not associated with differential activation of the DLPFC, as in studies of "cold" reasoning and explicit emotion regulation (suppression). Rather, it was associated with activations in the lateral and medial orbital PFC, ACC, insula, and the posterior cingulate and contiguous precuneus and parietal cortex. Neural information processing related to motivated reasoning appears to be qualitatively different from reasoning in the absence of a strong emotional stake in the conclusions reached. . . .

The large activation of the ventral striatum that followed subjects' processing of threatening information likely reflects reward or relief engendered by "successful" equilibration to an emotionally stable judgment. The combination of reduced negative affect (absence of activity in the insula and lateral orbital cortex) and increased positive affect or reward (ventral striatum activation) once subjects had ample time to reach biased conclusions suggests why motivated judgments may be so difficult to change (i.e., they are doubly reinforcing).

6. David McRaney, "The Illusion of Asymmetric Insight," August 21, 2011, blog entry, http://youarenotsosmart.com /2011/08/21/the-illusion-of-asymmetric-insight/.

Describing research by Emily Pronin, Lee Ross, Justin Kruger, and Kenneth Savitsky, McRaney writes:

> They had subjects identify themselves as either liberals or conservatives and in a separate run of the experiment as either pro-abortion and anti-abortion. The groups filled out questionnaires about their own beliefs and how they interpreted the beliefs of their opposition. They then rated how much insight their opponents possessed. The results showed liberals believed they knew more about conservatives than conservatives knew about liberals. The conservatives believed they knew more about liberals than liberals knew about conservatives. Both groups thought they knew more about their opponents than their opponents knew about themselves. The same was true of the pro-abortion rights and anti-abortion groups.
>
> The illusion of asymmetric insight makes it seem as though you know everyone else far better than they know you, and not only that, but you know them

better than they know themselves. You believe the same thing about groups of which you are a member. As a whole, your group understands outsiders better than outsiders understand your group, and you understand the group better than its members know the group to which they belong.

The researchers explained this is how one eventually arrives at the illusion of naïve realism, or believing your thoughts and perceptions are true, accurate and correct, therefore if someone sees things differently than you or disagrees with you in some way it is the result of a bias or an influence or a shortcoming. You feel like the other person must have been tainted in some way, otherwise they would see the world the way you do—the right way. The illusion of asymmetrical insight clouds your ability to see the people you disagree with as nuanced and complex. You tend to see yourself and the groups you belong to in shades of gray, but others and their groups as solid and defined primary colors lacking nuance or complexity.

In a political debate you feel like the other side just doesn't get your point of view, and if they could only see things with your clarity, they would understand

and fall naturally in line with what you believe. They must not understand, because if they did they wouldn't think the things they think. By contrast, you believe you totally get their point of view and you reject it. You see it in all its detail and understand it for what it is—stupid. You don't need to hear them elaborate. So, each side believes they understand the other side better than the other side understands both their opponents and themselves.

This leads me to interpret the "motivation" in motivated reasoning as tribal in nature. We want to raise our status in a tribe.

7. Tyler Cowen and Robin Hanson, "Are Disagreements Honest?," August 18, 2004, http://mason.gmu.edu/~rhanson /deceive.pdf.

The authors pose a puzzle. If you and I are both truth seekers, and we disagree, how should we take into account one another's opinions? After reviewing previous analyses showing that our opinions ought to converge, Cowen and Hanson conclude that the most likely reason that disagreement persists is that we are not truth seekers. This analysis is consistent with the psychologists' notion of motivated reasoning. I believe that it provides further reason to consider a model in which political opinions can be driven by tribal loyalty and status seeking.

8. Bryan Caplan, *The Myth of the Rational Voter: Why Democracies Choose Bad Policies* (Princeton: Princeton University Press, 2007).

One of the important arguments in this book is that it is rational not to invest much effort in formulating sound political opinions. I infer that a political ideology may, like a peacock's tail, be an elaborate signal that otherwise serves no practical function. Of course, I hope that things are not quite that bad, and that there is in fact a role for constructive reasoning to play.

9. Jeffrey Friedman, "Ignorance as a Starting Point: From Modest Epistemology to Realistic Political Theory," *Critical Review* 19, no. 1 (2007): 1–22.

Friedman takes us on a tour of the theory of political opinion formation, starting with a classic 1964 article by Philip Converse. An important distinction is between elite opinion and mass opinion. I limit the application of the three-axes model to the former, which is why I refer constantly to articulate, politically engaged contemporary Americans.

Notes

1. John Mauldin, "The Day After," Mauldin Economics website, "Outside the Box" investment newsletter, November 9, 2016, http://www.mauldineconomics.com/outsidethebox/the-day-after.

2. Originally, I used the term "freedom-coercion axis," but a reader, Declan Byrne, pointed out that freedom is embedded in all three axes, while liberty is more closely associated with the libertarian axis.

3. John Tooby, "Coalitional Instincts," Edge.org website, 2017, https://www.edge.org/response-detail/27168.

4. Paul Cassell, "The Physical Evidence in the Michael Brown Case Supported the Officer," *Washington Post*, November 28, 2014, https://www.washingtonpost.com/news/volokh-conspiracy/wp/2014/11/28/the-physical-evidence-in-the-michael-brown-case-supported-the-officer/.

5. Alicia H. Munnell, Lynn E. Browne, James McEneaney, and Geoffrey M. B. Tootell, "Mortgage Lending in Boston: Interpreting HMDA Data," Working Paper no. 92-7, Federal Reserve Bank of Boston, October 1992, https://www.bostonfed.org/-/media/Documents/Workingpapers/PDF/wp92_7.pdf.

6. Note, however, that Gary Johnson, presidential candidate of the Libertarian Party in 2012 and 2016, took the progressive position on this issue.

7. Catherine Rampell, "Britain's Flat Idea to Tax Soda and Other Sugary Drinks," *Washington Post*, March 22, 2016, https://www.washingtonpost.com/opinions/britains-flat-idea-to-tax-soda-and-other-sugary-drinks/2016/03/21/186e3ad0-efa1-11e5-89c3-a647fcce95e0_story.html.

8. Gary Klein, "Decentering," Edge.org website, 2017, https://www.edge.org/response-detail/27119.

9. David Corn, "Secret Video: Romney Tells Millionaire Donors What He Really Thinks of Obama Voters," *Mother Jones*, September 17, 2012, http://www.motherjones.com/politics/2012/09/secret-video-romney-private-fundraiser.

10. See for example, Pew Research Center, "Partisanship and Political Animosity in 2016," June 22, 2016, http://www.people-press.org/2016/06/22/partisanship-and-political-animosity-in-2016/.

11. Lee Rainie and Aaron Smith, "Main Findings," Pew Research Center, March 12, 2012, http://www.pewinternet.org/2012/03/12/main-findings-10/.

12. Robert Nozick, *Anarchy, State, and Utopia* (New York: Basic Books, 2013 [1974]), p. 247.

13. See, for example, Sagar A. Pandit and Carel P. van Schaik, "A Model for Leveling Coalitions among Primate Males: Toward a Theory of Egalitarianism," *Behavioral Ecology and Sociobiology* 55 (2003): 161–68, http://tuvalu.santafe.edu/~bowles/Dominance/Papers/Pandit%26vanSchaik'03.pdf.

14. *Overcoming Bias* blog; "Status Hypocrisy," blog entry by Robin Hanson, January 20, 2017, http://www.overcomingbias.com/tag/hypocrisy.

15. Tyler Cowen and Robin Hanson, "Are Disagreements Honest?" (Dept. of Economics, George Mason University), August 18, 2004, http://mason.gmu.edu/~rhanson/deceive.pdf.

16. Robert Nisbet, *The Quest for Community* (New York: Oxford University Press, 1969 [1953]); Daniel B. Klein, "The People's Romance: Why People Love Government (as Much as They Do)," *The Independent Review* 10, no. 1 (Summer 2005): 5–37.

17. Jason Tucker and Jason VandenBeukel, "'We're Teaching University Students Lies'—An Interview with Dr. Jordan Peterson," *C2C Journal*, December 1, 2016, http://www.c2cjournal.ca/2016/12/were-teaching-university-students-lies-an-interview-with-dr-jordan-peterson/.

18. Jordan B. Peterson, "2016 Maps of Meaning" lectures, https://www.youtube.com/playlist?list=PL22J3VaeABQAGbKJNDrRa6GNL0iL4KoOj.

19. Dylan Evans, "Need for Closure," Edge.org website, 2017, https://www.edge.org/response-detail/27101.

20. David McRaney, "The Illusion of Asymmetric Insight," *You Are Not So Smart: A Celebration of Self Delusion* (blog), August 21, 2011, https://youarenotsosmart.com/2011/08/21/the-illusion-of-asymmetric-insight/.

21. Jason Brennan, *Libertarianism: What Everyone Needs to Know* (New York: Oxford University Press, 2012), pp. 6–7.

22. Matthew D. Lieberman, "Naïve Realism," Edge.org website, 2017, https://www.edge.org/response-detail/27006.

23. Michael Anton, "The Flight 93 Election," The Claremont Institute, September 5, 2016, https://www.claremont.org/crb/basicpage/the-flight-93-election/.

24. Remarks by President Trump to the People of Poland, July 6, 2017, https://www.whitehouse.gov/briefings-statements/remarks-president-trump-people-poland/.

25. See, for example, Marc A. Thiessen, "Trump's Warsaw Speech Wasn't an Outrage. It Was a Clear Statement of American Values," The American Enterprise Institute, http://www.aei.org/publication/trumps-warsaw-speech-wasnt-an-outrage-it-was-a-clear-statement-of-american-values/.

26. See, for example, Peter Beinart, "The Racial and Religious Paranoia of Trump's Warsaw Speech," *Atlantic*, July 6, 2017, https://www.theatlantic.com/international/archive/2017/07/trump-speech-poland/532866/.

27. See, for example, Matt Welch, "Trump's Narrow View of 'Civilization'," *Reason*, July 6, 2017, https://reason.com/blog/2017/07/06/trumps-cramped-view-of-civilization.

28. Andrew Sullivan, "America Wasn't Built for Humans," *New York*, September 2017, http://nymag.com/intelligencer/2017/09/can-democracy-survive-tribalism.html?gtm=top&gtm=bottom.

29. Jonathan Haidt, "The Age of Outrage," City Journal, December 17, 2017, https://www.city-journal.org/html/age-outrage-15608.html

30. C. Thi Ngyuen, "Escape the Echo Chamber," Aeon, April 9, 2018, https://aeon.co/essays/why-its-as-hard-to-escape-an-echo-chamber-as-it-is-to-flee-a-cult.

31. Lilliana Mason, *Uncivil Agreement: How Politics Became Our Identity* (Chicago: University of Chicago Press, 2018), p. 21.

32. Sullivan, "America Wasn't Built for Humans."

33. Mason, *Uncivil Agreement*, p. 22.

34. Marc Hetherington and Jonathan Weiler, *Prius or Pickup?: How the Answers to Four Simple Questions Explain America's Great Divide* (New York: Houghton Mifflin Harcourt, 2018), pp. 128–129.

35. Ben Sasse, *Them: Why We Hate Each Other—and How to Heal* (New York: St. Martin's Press, 2018).

36. Ben Sasse, "Politics Can't Solve Our Political Problems," *Wall Street Journal*, October 12, 2018, https://www.wsj.com/articles/politics-cant-solve-our-political-problems-1539364986.

Index

Note: Information in notes is indicated by n.

About the Author

Arnold Kling received his PhD in economics from MIT in 1980. He is the author of several books, including *Crisis of Abundance: Rethinking How We Pay for Health Care*, published by the Cato Institute. He writes a monthly column for the Library of Economics and Liberty.

Find him online at www.arnoldkling.com.

Libertarianism.org

Liberty. It's a simple idea and the linchpin of a complex system of values and practices: justice, prosperity, responsibility, toleration, cooperation, and peace. Many people believe that liberty is the core political value of modern civilization itself, the one that gives substance and form to all the other values of social life. They're called libertarians.

Libertarianism.org is the Cato Institute's treasury of resources about the theory and history of liberty. The book you're holding is a small part of what Libertarianism.org has to offer. In addition to hosting classic texts by historical libertarian figures and original articles from modern-day thinkers, Libertarianism.org publishes podcasts, videos, online introductory courses, and books on a variety of topics within the libertarian tradition.

Cato Institute

Founded in 1977, the Cato Institute is a public policy research foundation dedicated to broadening the parameters of policy debate to allow consideration of more options that are consistent with the principles of limited government, individual liberty, and peace. To that end, the Institute strives to achieve greater involvement of the intelligent, concerned lay public in questions of policy and the proper role of government.

The Institute is named for *Cato's Letters*, libertarian pamphlets that were widely read in the American Colonies in the early 18th century and played a major role in laying the philosophical foundation for the American Revolution.

Despite the achievement of the nation's Founders, today virtually no aspect of life is free from government encroachment. A pervasive intolerance for individual rights is shown by government's arbitrary intrusions into private economic transactions and its disregard for civil liberties. And while freedom around the globe has notably increased in the past several decades, many countries have moved in the opposite direction, and most governments still do not respect or safeguard the wide range of civil and economic liberties.

To address those issues, the Cato Institute undertakes an extensive publications program on the complete spectrum of policy issues. Books, monographs, and shorter studies are commissioned to examine the federal budget, Social Security, regulation, military spending, international trade, and myriad other issues. Major policy conferences are held throughout the year, from which papers are published thrice yearly in the *Cato Journal*. The Institute also publishes the quarterly magazine *Regulation*.

In order to maintain its independence, the Cato Institute accepts no government funding. Contributions are received from foundations, corporations, and individuals, and other revenue is generated from the sale of publications. The Institute is a nonprofit, tax-exempt, educational foundation under Section 501(c)3 of the Internal Revenue Code.

CATO INSTITUTE

1000 Massachusetts Avenue, NW

Washington, DC 20001

www.cato.org